FLAG ON DEVIL'S ISLAND

FLAG ON DEVIL'S ISLAND

By

Francis Lagrange

With

William Murray

DOUBLEDAY & COMPANY, INC., GARDEN CITY, NEW YORK

1961

Devil's Island and St. Joseph, as seen from the shore line of Royale.

To protect the innocent, as well as the guilty, many of the names and some of the events of this narrative have been disguised.

Contents

Preface		vii
1.	An Unexpected Reunion	1
2.	The Ghosts of Devil's Island	9
3.	The Right Man in the Right Place	22
4.	The Best Intentions	31
5.	Respectability	40
6.	Enter Ludwig van Beethoven	50
7.	Crime Never Pays Enough	61
8.	Fra Bartolo	75
9.	Article 139	89
10.	The End of a Road	98

11. Hello, St. Laurent, Good-by 104

12. Dutch Treat 122

13. Monsieur Tronoir 133

14. The Bagne 138

15. Tourism, Third Class 151

16. The Islands 170

17. Crimes and Criminals 177

18. And So We Leave Beautiful Royale. . . . 188

19. March or Die! 197

20. Liquidation 211

21. The Last Fling 219

22. Cayenne 235

Color Plates

Devil's Island and St. Joseph.   (frontispiece)

New arrivals from the mainland.   (facing page 20)

A new load of convicts from France.   (facing page 21)

Below decks.   (facing page 52)

Arrival in St. Laurent.   (facing page 53)

Marching into St. Laurent for the first time.   (facing page 84)

Inside the camp.   (facing page 85)

A well-organized escape.   (facing page 116)

Disciplinary prison courts.   (facing page 117)

Punishment cells.   (facing page 148)

Solitary confinement on St. Joseph.   (facing page 149)

Life inside the barracks.   (facing page 180)

Sharks around the islands.   (facing page 181)

In the camps around St. Jean.   (facing page 212)

Rehabilitation?   (facing page 213)

Preface

BECAUSE of the unusual nature of this book, it may be of some value to the reader to know how it came to be written and published. The first person from the outside world to become interested in Francis Lagrange, in his work and his story, was an American public relations executive from Chicago named Richard S. Smith. Here is his own account of the events:

"In March 1959, I was in Caracas on business. When this business was completed, I decided, as a lark, to take a side trip to French Guiana and visit the French penal colony about which I had read considerably as a boy. When I reached Cayenne, the capital, I discovered that, though the prison had been closed in 1946, a large number of ex-Devil's Island convicts were still living in Guiana. I decided to interview some of them for a possible magazine article. During the process of going from one saloon to another and talking to these human derelicts, I found Lagrange sitting alone at a table in a tiny café on the waterfront. He was slightly drunk on *tafia*, the local rum, but he was able to narrate a portion of his life story to me. When he told me that he was an artist, I decided to visit his tiny studio and take a look at his work.

"Most of his canvases were landscapes, primitive paintings of bush Negroes, Indians, etc. But his best work, he said, was a collection of paintings he had begun while in solitary confinement on the islands (Devil's Island). These were scenes of life as it was in the penal colony.

"He did not own these paintings, however. They had been sold, all twenty-four of them, and presently were hanging in an old restaurant, the proprietor of which was also an ex-convict, a few miles outside Cayenne.

"We drove out to see them. There they were, gathering dust around the walls of the room. The proprietor would not sell *one* painting. He would sell only the entire collection, for which he wanted a substantial sum.

"Not having enough cash with me, I decided merely to take photos of the paintings with the idea of trying to sell them back in the States.

"I must have shown these photos to 500 different people, all of whom were very interested, but not sufficiently to finance their purchase. Finally, I showed the photos to Mr. Bailey K. Howard, president of Field Enterprises Educational Corporation in Chicago. He agreed to buy them almost immediately and also agreed to advance the necessary funds to send me back to Cayenne. Carmen Reporto, a photographer on the staff of the Chicago *Sun-Times*, was assigned to accompany me and act as Mr. Howard's agent on the transaction."

Smith and Reporto brought the paintings back to Chicago and turned them over to Bailey Howard, who was amazed by their quality and deeply moved by their subject matter. The pictures are rather crude in color, because of the materials Lagrange was forced to work with and the circumstances under which they were painted, but they are marvelously alive, full of fascinating pictorial details, and obviously the work of a skilled artist. Furthermore, they are the only authentic pictorial record of life in the penal colonies of French Guiana, since the authorities had never permitted photographers to enter the prisons or even to photograph the inmates working as trustees outside the various camps. Lagrange was the only man who could have left us such a record because, as he put it himself, he was "the only artist in residence at the time." Fifteen of the twenty-four pictures are reproduced in this book.

During their stay in Cayenne, Smith and Reporto had further occasion to talk to Lagrange and they discovered that he had already begun to write about his experiences. They brought this news back with them along with the paintings and it was Reporto who suggested that such a book might be of interest to an American publisher. Howard agreed and got in touch with Doubleday.

There were a number of problems to be overcome. First of all, Lagrange said that he did not have the time or the energy to write the book by himself, being deeply engaged in his work as a painter. Secondly, he did not speak English and his manuscript would have to be translated. Thirdly, the editors of Doubleday felt that, even under the best of circumstances and with all the good will in the world, he would probably not be able to write the book by himself, since by his own admission he was not a professional writer. So, because I am lucky enough to be able to speak French with some fluency, I was hired and sent to Cayenne to help Lagrange write his story.

He turned out to be an extraordinary man with an extraordinary story to tell. After working closely with him over a period of many weeks, there is no question in my mind but that he could have written the book by himself, though in French, of course. He is an educated, cultured man with a lively interest in the world around him, an insatiable reader, and a

witty critic of past and current events. More important, he has
the real writer's ability to tell a story well and a wonderful
ear for language. After the first two or three difficult days, in
which we were feeling each other out as people, we enjoyed
a perfect collaboration based on a mutual respect for each
other's abilities. This is not an "as told to" book. I organized it
and did much of the descriptive writing, but the events are
narrated in what I hope is the English equivalent of Lagrange's
own words and the point of view is uniquely his.

WILLIAM MURRAY

FLAG ON DEVIL'S ISLAND

1 An Unexpected Reunion

*E*VEN during my comparatively brief but happy fling as a highly successful criminal, I have always been a creature of regular habits. I like to get up at a certain hour, work a certain set period of time, eat and drink on schedule, see my friends and mistresses daily and my enemies only when my liver makes it absolutely necessary for me to be irritable with someone. I rarely stick to any one schedule very long—usually the pressure of circumstances forces me to alter it—but I inevitably settle into a new one and adjust chronometrically, with a minimum of discomfort. The approach, you see, has always been casual, never hysterical. I do not try to impose myself on life; I always fit quietly into it, like a tired foot into a comfortable old shoe. Perhaps this is why I never had the slightest difficulty in adjusting to the monotonous routines of prison existence, even during the fifteen years I served in the notorious penal colonies of French Guiana.

I have to admit that my schedules would doubtless strike most people as bizarre—I now like to paint only between 7 and 11 A.M., I believe in love in the afternoon, and I eat once a day, at midnight—but I am sixty-eight years old, often a little tired, and I suit myself.

I have always been an artist as well as a criminal and I
believe in the present, so I ignore the future and I rarely think
about the past. But the past is there, of course, lurking un-
chained in the shadows of my memory, and occasionally,
goaded by the spur of some vivid, instantly recognizable image,
it rushes out to overwhelm me. I am not afraid of it nor do I
regret it. Above all, I would not deny it: I am what I have
always been, a man responsible for his own actions, and I have
always paid the prices demanded of those actions. But I do not
believe in the past, which is why I have never written about
it. Not until now, not until the goad to my memory became
too powerful to be resisted, not until the image itself appeared
in the form of a long-forgotten, dearly loved face.

It happened last summer during one of those sultry, breath-
less mornings that succeed each other endlessly during the long
dry season in Guiana. I had planted myself in front of my
easel at seven o'clock, right on schedule, but had been unable
to accomplish anything. I was working, I remember, on a large
nude, one of a series I was doing on the Indian tribes of the
Upper Maroni for the local tourist store. The nude, a flat-faced,
copper-colored princess with a sullen expression and pendulous
breasts, had resisted every attempt at improvement. The expression had grown more sullen, the breasts more pendulous,
and my liver more and more irascible. Finally, after several
hours of struggle and sweat, I abandoned the hideous princess,
changed into a dry shirt, walked out of my dark and hostile
little studio and into the noise, dirt, and heat of Cayenne at
midday. I consoled myself with the thought that I was still almost on schedule, since every day, at about this time, I was in
the habit of stopping by the café for my usual chat and
apéritif with my friends.

The café is around the corner from where I live, right in

the heart of Cayenne, the capital of French Guiana, and it is the only one of its kind in the whole country. It is run by an overworked white couple from the *métropole* who are very anxious to please everyone and make a great success of their venture. *Monsieur* remains in the kitchen, where he cooks solid, tasty French provincial dishes, and *Madame* supervises events from behind the bar and counts the money. The interior is cool and crowded with square tables covered with white cloths, and outside, on the sidewalk, one sits at tiny round tables and stares at the varied, colorful world moving by, a time-honored French custom. I am not modest and I think I can say that what differentiates this *café* from all the others in Cayenne, quite apart from the superiority of the food, are the splendid murals I painted for it. There is a map of Guiana, copiously illustrated in several colors; there are Indians, Creoles, bush Negroes, some sketches of old friends from prison days, scenes of animal and plant life, and always, in every picture, the feeling of the jungle that surrounds us, that *is* Guiana. *Monsieur* and *Madame* are people of taste, they acknowledge and rejoice in their world, they are *French*, and that is why I always come to their café to have my *apéritif* and my morning chat.

On this particular day I was too discouraged to do more than barely acknowledge the greetings of my friends and acquaintances and I sat down by myself at the only remaining empty sidewalk table, just under the edge of the long awning shielding the viewers from the tropical sun. I was very much alone in all that crowd, alone with my gloomy thoughts and feelings, insensitive for once to the bustle of people moving ceaselessly past my chair. I was an old man, I could no longer paint, and I was quite prepared to spend the rest of my life right there, suffering.

Suddenly, I became conscious of a large pair of shoes. They

were standing directly in front of my table. I looked slowly up, up along the whole length of a spotless army uniform, and into the kind, smiling face of a handsome young man. There was something terribly, pleasingly familiar about that face, but the uniform disturbed me, as uniforms will. My experiences with uniforms have rarely been beneficial to me. So I concentrated on the uniform and tried to ignore the face. "Yes?" I snapped.

"You are Francis Lagrange, are you not?" the young man asked.

"Unfortunately."

"My name is Bonnard."

I was stunned, overwhelmed. "Bonnard?" I said, staring up at this robust, athletic-looking young man with the smiling countenance. "The son of Julien?"

"Yes, I am Paul Bonnard, my dear Flag," the young man said, addressing me by my nickname. "You don't recognize me, but I would have known you anywhere."

I stood up, took him by the shoulders, and looked at him. In that moment nothing else existed for me; Cayenne, the café, the people around us disappeared and I was transported twenty-two years into my past, back into one of the more bearable periods of my life as a convict on the *Îles du Salut*, the tiny island group known popularly to the outside world as Devil's Island.

For a long time I was unable to say anything and I could tell that Paul understood my emotion. After we had embraced each other in silence and I was finally able to speak, Paul sat down and we began to talk. We talked of our life on the islands, of the people we had known there, of the many things that had happened to each of us then and since. For this young man, now so mature, so nattily attired in the crisp, impressive uniform of a sergeant-major, had been, when I knew him best, a small, dirty, mischievous boy of eight, a regular Peter Pan.

His father, Julien Bonnard, then commandant of the penal administration on the islands, had called me into his office one day and entrusted the boy's education to me, since Paul had fallen badly behind at school and needed help. It was not unusual in those days for the better-educated convicts to be called upon to tutor the children of various penal functionaries. "Do what you can with him," *Monsieur* Bonnard had told me, "but I believe it's hopeless. The child is determined to remain ignorant."

For the better part of two years I had seen young Paul nearly every day. I had put up with his pranks, encouraged him, defended him even against his father, and all that time continued to stuff his unwilling head with French and German grammar. I even taught him how to draw, a talent he had immediately put to use by adding a mustache and a large beard to an unfinished Madonna I had thoughtlessly left behind on my easel one day. Despite or perhaps because of everything, I had come to love Paul, to love him as deeply as I had respected his father and admired his mother.

"And how is your father?" I asked him.

"He is old and ill and very frail," Paul said, "but he hasn't changed. He writes me very stern letters and tells me what to do and what not to do. It was my father, you know, who got me into the army."

I told him I didn't know and Paul brought me up to date. "You remember," he continued, "that, after the death of my mother, my father took my younger brother Jean and me back to France. He found good schools for us and boarded us out with relatives, then he came back to Guiana. But that was 1939 and the war caught us. When France fell, my father joined De Gaulle and we did not see him again for eight years. By that time I was seventeen and more of a savage than ever. My father was so appalled that he forced me to enlist. 'You're a bandit,' he told me. 'If you don't go into the army, you'll wind up in jail and I've had quite enough of convicts in my life!' So I joined the army and, to my surprise, I loved it."

Paul told me that he had always wanted to return to Guiana and that he was now stationed with the garrison in Cayenne, where he hoped to remain permanently. "And what about you, Flag?" he asked me. "How goes it with you?"

I shrugged and told him what little I could, that I was getting along reasonably well and earning my living as a painter; that some weeks it was slow, some weeks it went well, but that I could always paint for myself as well as for others. There was satisfaction in my life.

Paul smiled affectionately. "No more nonsense, Flag?"

I smiled back. "I am too old," I said, "and I'm enjoying my freedom."

"My father always described you as an old fox. Sympathetic, but incorrigible."

I laughed. "Your father is quite right," I told him. "I have always had this dreadful weakness for money."

"He said you were the greatest forger and counterfeiter in all France."

"I was certainly one of the greatest," I agreed.

"And you would do it all again?"

"I would try not to get caught," I said. "I have too much respect for your father."

We chatted and joked some more and then Paul went back to his duties. After that, I saw him nearly every day. We would bump into each other in the street or he would come up to my studio or we'd meet at the café for a drink. And each time was like that first reunion, a blinding moment of recognition followed by an onrush of so many sad and terrible and funny memories. Then one day, at the bar, Paul told me that he had just received another letter from his father. "He wants to know if I've been back to see my mother's grave."

"And have you?"

He shook his head, then glanced shyly at me. "I'd like you to come with me, Flag."

"No."

"You haven't ever been back to the islands?"

"Not since I was freed," I said. "More than fifteen years ago."

"Then you don't know what it's like today. Actually, I'm curious to see, aren't you?"

Of course I was, but I couldn't explain to young Paul that my curiosity was strongly tinged with fear and horror. After all, he had been only a boy and the son of the commandant at that; I had been on the islands as a prisoner and it had not always been as endurable as during those two years under his father's administration. Despite the enormous lies that have been told everywhere about the penal colonies of French Guiana, Devil's Island, so-called, had seen enough suffering and injustice to deserve, at least in part, its reputation. I had no desire to relive any of it. I had not been back since my own liberation in 1946 nor since the final closing down of the prisons in the early 1950s. I had been told that the jungle had already overrun most of the buildings and I think, too, that I was afraid of what I might hear in the silence of those cell blocks, now partly buried beneath a tangle of creepers and rustling vines. It wasn't that I didn't believe in my past; I realized that I was afraid of it.

"You will come with me, won't you?" Paul said, interrupting my gloomy thoughts. "I think my father would want you to."

I did not answer him right away, but I knew that I could not refuse him. The past could no longer be denied; I had been overwhelmed. I would have to face the ghosts I knew were waiting for me on the islands and to relive in vivid memory at least some portion of my strange life.

2 The Ghosts of Devil's Island

T_HE_ *îles du Salut,* or Salvation Islands, rise out of the deep blue of the South Atlantic about ten miles off the coast of Guiana and some thirty miles northwest of Cayenne. Ironically, in view of their later history and the world-wide notoriety of the penal colonies in general, the three small islands that make up the group are not only lovely to look at but benefit from an especially salubrious climate. In 1765, after a disastrous French attempt at colonization on the mainland directly opposite, at Kourou, in which 11,000 people died of various tropical diseases and privation in not quite two years, a few hundred survivors took refuge on the islands, where the fresh sea breezes and the absence of germ-carrying insects soon restored their health. Hence the name Salvation Islands. The largest of the group was called Royale, in honor of King Louis XV, who had dispatched the colonists to their deaths; the second largest, St. Joseph, after the patron saint of the expedition, who had clearly neglected his duties; and the smallest, so the story goes, Du Diable, or Devil's Island, because the refugees were prevented from landing on it by the strong, dangerous currents that swirl off its rocky coasts. And it is, of course, with this highly romantic name, Devil's Island, that the world has come to identify French justice.

I'd like to contribute my own little bit of historical interpretation right here, because I have a less glamorous theory as to how Devil's Island got its name. Though the currents around it are indeed strong and treacherous, it seems unfair to blame the devil. Nor is there anything particularly ominous about the place itself; it is certainly not the dry, barren rock people imagine it to be. Though tiny, being only about 1200 yards in circumference, the island is lush, covered with palm trees and a dense undergrowth of tropical foliage. In fact, it looks like a miniature paradise. But for hundreds of years the place has been a social center for flocks of blackbirds, who every summer, during the dry season, descend upon it by the thousands to feed on palm-tree blossoms and exchange gossip. These birds are large, noisy, and unpleasant creatures, and they are known locally as *oiseaux diables,* or devil birds. For some strange reason they have always ignored Royale and St. Joseph, where there are just as many palm trees, and gather only on Du Diable. I believe this phenomenon accounts more plausibly and truthfully for the naming of the island (the Indians, for instance, have always identified the bird with the area), though I am reluctant to dispel the fog of romance and glamour that for a hundred years has enshrouded the place. However, the idea of Devil's Island as a disease-ridden pesthole is only another in a long series of centuries-old popular misconceptions about Guiana in general, misconceptions that have characterized the whole history of this unfortunate, much maligned country.

In 1498, Columbus sailed off the coast of Guiana and touched down briefly at the Paria Peninsula, in what is now northeastern Venezuela. So some people began to think of this whole section of South America as "the land of the pariahs," a desolate waste fit only for outcasts. Then, in the sixteenth cen-

tury, the legend of El Dorado gripped the imagination of all
Europe. There was supposed to be a lost city somewhere in
the jungle, a metropolis whose streets were paved with gold
and diamonds, which was ruled by a wise, loving king who
washed himself each day in liquid gold. Spaniards died by the
thousands looking for it and slaughtered the helpless Indian
tribes in the search. In 1595, Walter Raleigh sailed up the
Orinoco after it and he never gave up; in 1617 he made his
last attempt and succeeded in ruining himself, decimating his
expedition and bringing about the death of his own son.

The French, though more skeptical about the existence of
El Dorado, were nevertheless convinced that Guiana itself was
a land of roses and wine. In 1626 they established a colony on
the coast at Sinnamary. It failed. They tried again elsewhere
in 1635, 1643, 1645, 1652, 1664, and 1674. Hardly anyone
survived. The huge expedition of 1763 was composed largely
of ruined nobles, dubious ladies in plumed hats, and unsuc-
cessful burghers from Alsace-Lorraine. They had been told
that all they had to do was lean over to pick up the gold. In
their hurry, they neglected to bring food or suitable equipment.
They died with astonishing rapidity. During the Revolution
boatloads of royalists were dumped to perish on the muddy
beaches, and in 1794 the followers of Robespierre joined them.
And, as if things weren't bad enough in the colony, there were
intermittent wars with the English, the Dutch, and the Portuguese. Somehow the French managed to lose them all.

It wasn't until the first half of the nineteenth century that
the colony began to enjoy an era of precarious prosperity. This
was due to the large-scale importation of African slaves, who
provided a cheap labor force for the newly established planters
of coffee and sugar. But unfortunately for commerce, we
French have always managed to pollute our genius for injus-

tice and colonial oppression with a damaging streak of pure
quixotism. In 1848 the government was afflicted with a rush
of humanity to the head and emancipated the slaves, most of
whom promptly quitted the plantations to live in squalor in the
towns or to resume a primitive tribal life in the bush. When
the hurried substitution of Asiatics also failed (instead of
drudging in the cane fields, the Chinese opened shops), France
embarked on "the white experiment."

In October 1851, Louis Napoleon signed the decree that
turned French Guiana into the site of a penal administration
and in May of the following year the initial shipment of convicts arrived on the *Îles du Salut,* where the first prisons were
organized. Later, over the course of the next few years, the central penal colonies were established on the mainland, at St.
Laurent and St. Jean on the Maroni River, which separates
French Guiana from Surinam (Dutch Guiana). There was
another large prison in Cayenne itself, and there were smaller,
isolated work camps scattered along the coast and throughout
the interior. The islands themselves were reserved for convicts
requiring special surveillance and punishment, the most common offense being attempts to escape from the mainland
camps. The prisoners were brought to Guiana at the rate of
two boatloads a year and during the boom decades of the administration, from about 1890 on, the settlements contained
approximately 6500 men. (From 1885 to 1902 the shipments
included women, but lurid scandals forced the discontinuance
of this policy of equal suffering among the sexes.)

The unwilling residents of the *bagne,* a slang term roughly
equivalent to the American phrase "the jug," were divided into
three main classifications: *condamnés,* convicts serving regular
prison sentences; *relégués,* criminals with four or more convic-
tions against them who were exiled permanently to the colony;

and *libérés*, men who had served their sentences but were still condemned to reside in Guiana. This latter classification can be explained by the admirable French institution of *doublage*, or doubling, a petty law that forced a man to live as many additional years in the penal colony as the length of his actual prison term. *Doublage* was the wholly unjust method by which the government intended to insure permanent colonization, an ideal doubtless inspired by the settling of convicts in Australia, but the white experiment failed as completely as the black and yellow ones. The economy of the country was still dependent on the working of the plantations, but men who had spent years in jungle work camps or in solitary confinement on the islands had no intention, once they were free, of slaving for low pay under a brutal sun. They preferred to remain in Cayenne or St. Laurent, the second-largest town, where they lived a hand-to-mouth existence in the streets. And, of course, the presence of a penal administration, like a spreading cancer through the whole country, effectively discouraged any voluntary economic development from France itself. The misconception by which it was hoped to solve the economic problems of Guiana through "the white experiment" was probably the most idiotic and costly of the whole series. Thirty years after the creation of the *bagne*, the jungle had overrun the plantations and the economy of the country had been brought to a total standstill, a situation that still persists today, though there have been some recent indications of a change for the better.

It was the famous case of Alfred Dreyfus that, in 1894, first focused the attention of the outside world on the goings-on in French Guiana. Sentenced to life imprisonment for allegedly betraying his country and banished to Devil's Island, where he spent five dismal years under the fanatically watchful eyes of five personal guards, Dreyfus came to symbolize through his unjust suffering the corruption of an entire society, and the tiny island on which he lived in terrible isolation lent its sinister name permanently to the whole vast complex of the penal administration. Even today, most people outside of France don't realize that the prisons in Guiana no longer exist, and they believe that Devil's Island was and is the single specific place where the sadistic French send prisoners to be tortured and killed. Another misconception, but, for once, a beneficial one since it eventually led to the abolition of the *bagne*.

When I first saw the famous islands in 1934 and took up unwilling residence there, they were crowded, busy places. Royale and St. Joseph, though considerably larger than Du Diable, are each only about a mile and a quarter around and at the time they accommodated a total of about 800 prisoners, plus another several hundred guards and functionaries. Royale was the site of the main prison, which housed about 500 convicts who had either tried to escape or had been sent to the islands for such minor infractions as fighting, stealing, or insubordination. The commandant lived on Royale, and the central administrative buildings, the hospital, and the church were all there. So was the guillotine, devoted to a settling of accounts with those convicts who had murdered someone—a guard, a civilian, an Indian, a fellow prisoner. St. Joseph was the home of the *incos*, the incorrigibles, men sentenced to several years of solitary confinement or awaiting the day of execution on Royale. As for Devil's Island, it had, since Dreyfus, been reserved exclusively for political prisoners, and, at the time of my arrival, I believe there were six men on it. They lived in tiny, solitary huts among the trees, entirely cut off from the rest of us, doomed like Dreyfus to pace the shore line and stare interminably out to sea.

In those days, you went to the islands in a small, coastal steamer. It dropped anchor off Royale and you could stare through a barred porthole at the green, peaceful-looking slopes rising out of a calm, very blue sea. Eventually, a boat would come away from the shore and soon you would find yourself in it, surrounded by other convicts, being rowed toward the tiny harbor of Royale. The closer you came to the islands, the more strikingly beautiful they seemed—three rounded peaks soaring out of the ocean, the brilliant, almost waxy green of jungle foliage pierced by the shimmering light of white walls, the glare softened by rust-colored rooftops, the entire scene bathed in bright sunlight and hugged between the dark-blue of water and the lighter tint of a cloudless sky. As a painter I could not but respond to the scene, and I even remember being struck by the gay contrast in motion we convicts made in our red-and-white striped suits against that background of green and white trapped between sky and sea. I've tried to put that feeling of strong, basic color into all my paintings, because the colors of the islands and of Guiana in general are like that— brilliant, dazzling, merciless, primeval.

Approaching the islands again with Paul, after so many years, the colors were all still there, but the contrasts had changed. Leaning against the railing of the small motor launch in which we had set out from Cayenne early that morning, I again saw the islands rising out of the sea to meet me. At first they looked much the same, but then, as we came closer, I noticed the changes. The green was stronger, predominant, almost unrelieved, especially on St. Joseph; the jungle was reclaiming its own. The buildings no longer pierced the foliage in brilliant white, but seemed to peek out, as if struggling vainly against the surge of an engulfing tide. As we skirted the shore line of St. Joseph, I could barely make out the dim, now gray-white shapes of barracks and cell blocks. Then, between St. Joseph and Royale, a fierce, tidal current pushed against us and I saw the surge of green above the black rocks of Du Diable, a swift glimpse before we glided into the calm, still water below Royale.

On Royale, the buildings were still there, plainly visible, but surely doomed in their turn to vanish. The small cement pier had been partly washed away and our launch bumped lightly against a tumble of black, slippery boulders over which we scrambled ashore. To our right, the black, yawning arches of what had once been the bakery; to our left, the jungle closed in and the island above was hidden from view. A narrow, twisting path led off through the bush and up the slopes. And suddenly I could only stand there, paralyzed, as the ghosts rushed out to meet me.

"What's wrong, Flag?" Paul asked. He had started up the path and had turned back to look at me.

"The silence," I said. "Listen to the silence."

Paul noticed it, too, but it had not struck him as forcibly, so that I almost felt unable to breathe. In that silence I heard the voices of a thousand men; heard the bustle of coming and going around the harbor and the bakery; the shouts of workers gathering coconuts or clambering over the rocks after shellfish or sea turtles; the march of feet over the packed earth of courtyards and roads; the sharp, staccato barks of the guards; the soft clinking of chains; the grating of cell doors opening and closing; the scrape of keys turning in a hundred locks; the clamor of the camp bell tolling out our duties for the day and the deeper pealing of the one above the church, summoning us to pray for our own damned souls; the sound of a gun fired out over the water and the scream of a man hit, dying; the soft, sudden, deadly whoosh and thud of the guillotine. These were the sounds I heard in that silence as I stood there after so many years, after all that time and all those events. I could not move.

Finally, after several minutes, I collected my wits and Paul and I began the slow climb into my past. The ghosts were everywhere. I saw them in faces peering out from the windows of the guards' barracks and the bungalows of functionaries. By the ruins of the commandant's house, with its view over the sea and the harbor below, Paul and I felt the presence of his father, seated impassively as usual behind his desk. We climbed the steps of the hospital, pushing aside the foliage, and stood in the silent waiting room below the sagging of cracked walls and caved-in ceilings. I went into one of the smaller reception rooms for patients and found some of my drawings, satirical sketches I had done on one wall of prisoners being examined or about to undergo treatment at the hands of an eager surgeon clutching a huge bone saw. Beyond the hospital, we passed a wild pig rooting among rotten coconut shells in what had once been the priest's garden and then we came to the steps of the church itself. Here I hesitated again, because I was truly afraid of what I would find inside, but Paul took my arm and in we went.

Perhaps because the building is located at the highest point of the island, on a comparatively barren area exposed to wind and weather, the jungle had been held at bay. Though grass was pushing up through the stone floor, the inside of the church was free of the crush of vegetation that was strangling and demolishing the other buildings. Paul and I stood in the doorway and gazed up through the dim light over several rows of rotting pews to the dark wood of the altar, dusty with cobwebs, then up to the surrounding walls. Paul squeezed my arm. "You see, Flag," he whispered, "they are still there!"

It was true. My paintings, my murals were still there. Speechless, staring up at them, I realized that what I had feared most from this trip was not finding them again. I had spent so many months painting them, had devoted so much love to them, that a part of me had been left behind forever on the island when I had gone. Slowly, I circled the floor, making a full survey, trying to estimate how much longer the pictures could survive the dampness, the wind, the subtle destruction of time. Not long, I decided, though only the large angels I had painted below the railing of the balcony were in an advanced stage of decay. Still, all of the pictures were peeling and I knew it would probably be my very last chance to see what I am convinced is the best work I've ever done.

I am not basically a religious man, since my attitude to life has always been pliant and afflicted by a certain impatience with those who have blind faith in the unknown, but I believe that the one time I have been close to some understanding of the mystery was during the period I spent painting these perhaps old-fashioned re-creations of Biblical scenes. I had known what was wanted in that church—something simple, images readily available to simple minds—and I had begun to paint them with a certain cynicism, until soon something in the work itself engrossed me. I remember weeks of furious, concentrated labor, when, high on a scaffolding à la Michelangelo, I was lost to the world of men, in the grip of some cosmic force out of which, tirelessly, my hands were creating the story of man's spiritual life. I painted saints and angels, Christ and the holy family, the disciples, the hosts of heaven and earth. At work in the church on Royale, I had forgotten that I was a convicted criminal, an outcast among outcasts, and I had been brought face to face with the real meaning and purpose of my life. I had been an artist, expressing in his work the purest part of himself. This, I think, is perhaps the heart of all mystery and religion. I don't know. I only know what I felt and what these paintings, even today, mean to me.

It was some time before I noticed that Paul had gone. I went out through the rear of the church, forcing myself away from the paintings, and I found him standing waist-deep among the weeds of the little cemetery in which his mother lies. Silently, we placed a few blossoms on her grave, then walked back toward the church. But I did not want to go back inside again because I was afraid of caring too much about what was happening to my pictures, abandoned to oblivion on those rotting walls, so we skirted the building, went back past the hospital, hacked our way through thick bush, and soon found ourselves in a narrow, walled courtyard beside the long, low shape of a cell block.

Paul wanted to move on, but I knew where I was and I began a slow, methodical search for the spot. After a few minutes, I found it. I kicked the vegetation aside and my foot scraped across two parallel stone slabs embedded in the ground. Here the guillotine had stood. I looked at the slabs, then turned away, pushed aside a forest of vines, walked down a short flight of steps and into the cell block. Paul remained outside. I crept slowly along the wall of the corridor until I came to Cell 16.

The door was ajar, permanently rusted into this half-open position. I peered around it and gazed in. Even my bed was still there, flat against one wall, the foot of it almost up against the doorway. The small, round hole high up against the ceiling still let in a few rays of dim light. A large, hairy spider scampered away across the floor. I shut my eyes and stood face to face with my own ghost.

I was stretched out on that narrow bed, propped up against

the wall, one shoulder twisted away from it so that I could have the full benefit of what light there was. On my lap lay a shred of canvas, resting its weight against a broken board, and my face leaned down, down, my right hand moving slowly against the cloth. Here, sentenced to three months of solitary confinement for insubordination, I had begun to paint my story of life in the *bagne*. I had bribed a guard to provide the canvas, the board, the brushes, and the small amounts of ordinary house paint he had been able to obtain. And this was how I had worked, hour after hour, until my shoulder ached and my arm grew numb and the light from the hole above had faded. Out of those beginnings had grown my series of pictures of convicts and convict life. It had saved me from going mad during the long, dismal days when the sounds of life outside were torture to a caged, isolated man. I don't even remember that guard's name now, but I think of him as a saint.

Paul called to me from the courtyard and I opened my eyes. The cell was empty. Outside, a breeze stirred the tops of the palm trees and the creepers rustled against the walls of the building. I did not move for another second or two, then I swiftly turned and walked out of that place for the very last time.

Not speaking, each of us alone with his own memories, we left the cell block and pushed our way down the far slopes of the island through the thick bush until we came out into another windswept clearing. To our left, far below us, the sea washed against the rocks and beyond the swift current of the channel Devil's Island baked in the hot sun, a wall of hard green seemingly suspended in endless blue. Ahead of us was a knoll encircled by the crumbling ramparts of a stone wall; from there a cable had connected Royale to Devil's Island, the easiest method of getting supplies across to the politicals. We climbed the knoll and looked down on Du Diable, then

New arrivals from the mainland were rowed ashore in boats manned entirely by bagnards.

straight across at St. Joseph. The water between the islands
flowed on, unbroken for the moment by the black, cutting fins
of sharks. The tide had not yet fully turned or we would have
seen them as all of us on the islands had always seen them—
their silent, menacing shapes in swift pursuit of the schools of
smaller fish that moved, feeding, with the tidal currents. The
silence of the place hung like a weight in the air around us
and we paused there again to listen to it. Then, at last, from
the other side of the island we heard the distant sound of a
human voice calling, followed at once by the insistent whining of the launch's siren. It was our signal to return to the
boat. The trip back to Cayenne would take three hours, more
if the tide was running against us, and it was getting late.

All the way back to the harbor, Paul and I did not look at
each other. As we stumbled over the rocks toward the launch,
Paul said, "I'm sorry, Flag."

I shrugged impatiently. "Sorry? Why?"

"I did not know," he said. "I didn't think what it could mean
to you."

He would have continued, but I stopped him. "Nonsense,"
I said. "I'm glad we came. I've always wondered about coming
back to the islands, what I'd find here. I'm glad we came."

"You are?"

"Yes, I've seen myself very clearly. It was worth it."

We climbed into the boat and I sat down on the floor with
my back to Royale. Soon I felt the engine pulling us away from
the ruined pier. I smoked a cigarette and idly watched St.
Joseph slide past. Then I stared at my feet and finished the
cigarette. When I couldn't stand it any longer, I turned
around. The islands were already blurred shapes behind me,
but the voices of my ghosts had become increasingly audible.
I listened, not without some pleasure.

Twice a year the prison ship La Martinière
*sailed from France with a new load of con-
victs.*

3 The Right Man in the Right Place

I WAS standing in front of a desk, trying not to fidget and listening to the calm, emotionless voice of the man sitting behind it. "Lagrange, I've heard a good deal about you," the voice was saying. "That's why I sent for you."

"Yes, sir."

"I've been told that you're as big a rogue as any of the others here on Royale," the voice said, "but cleverer than most."

I started to protest, but a thin, almost emaciated hand rose off the desk and waved me into silence. The voice continued: "And I'm also aware that you are a charming and magnificent liar."

I shrugged. "I do what I can, sir."

"How long have you been on Royale, Lagrange?"

The voice had acquired a slight edge and I answered carefully. "Not quite five months this tour, sir."

"Three of which you have just passed in solitary confinement for insubordination."

"Yes, sir."

"That does not speak highly for your brains."

"No, sir."

There was a slight pause before the interview continued. I

concentrated on my expression of blank innocence and waited. A pair of ice-blue eyes stared directly into mine and then the cold voice resumed: "And I also understand that you are formidably talented as a painter."

"I do my best, sir," I answered casually, but my knees stiffened. I thought I knew what was coming and I was already fabricating plausible-sounding answers. I was not anxious to return to that cell for another three months.

"So talented, in fact, that you are able to paint under the most difficult conditions," the voice said. "Even in the dark."

Well, I thought, there's nothing to do now but brave it out. The bastard knows and I've always made a point of being charming in adversity. "Not in the dark, sir," I said. "I could paint hanging from the ceiling like a bat, I'm sure, but not in the dark."

Another pause while the eyes surveyed me. There was an odd glint in them and I wasn't sure what it meant. "Well, Lagrange," the voice said at last, "I think you can have the light you need. As for hanging from the ceiling, you may find you have to do exactly that." I stared at him. "Go up and talk to Father Perrier. He wants you to decorate the church. It's not a bad idea, is it? It may even keep you out of mischief."

I stood there like an imbecile, trying to collect my wits. I had been wanting to paint inside that church ever since my first week on the island and my initial glimpse of all that virgin wall space. I opened my mouth to say something, then shut it again.

"That's all, Lagrange," the voice snapped. I turned to go and got as far as the door. "Lagrange?"

"Yes, sir?"

"I've seen some of your work."

"Sir?"

"The paintings you've been doing in the solitude of your private room."

"Oh."

"They're very good, Lagrange. You must finish them some day."

"Yes, sir."

"Try to stay out of trouble and then you won't have to corrupt my guards to get your work done."

"Yes, sir," I said and walked out of the room in a daze.

That was my first meeting with Julien Bonnard, the new commandant of the islands, and it was typical of the man. I don't know how others may remember him. I suspect that more than a few of my fellow convicts would speak badly of him. They might say that he was "a rough one," a tyrant, a rascal, a weasel. I don't know. What prison warden has ever been universally loved by his charges? As for me, all I can say is that he was the right man in the right place.

And why? Because he knew, above all, how to deal with the *bagnards*. He understood us and he spoke our language, whether we were peasants, illiterates, sophisticates, hooligans, thugs, or college professors. He had something of our own to say to each one of us and his method of treating us varied with each individual. He had risen rapidly through the hierarchy of the penal administration, achieving the rank of commandant in only eight years. If he had been entrusted with governing the islands, the most delicate and difficult job of all, it was because he was supremely fitted for the post.

He was not only astute and subtle in his dealings with the convicts; he was equally skillful in dealing with his personnel. Most of the guards, perhaps seventy per cent of them, were Corsicans. They were tough, silent, ignorant men, fundamentally loyal only to one another and capable of the most extreme brutality and duplicity. Bonnard could handle them because he had grasped their psychology; he would not trample on their curious private code of blood brotherhood and vengeance. He had succeeded, without loving or being loved by them, in being respected and obeyed.

He was always on the move, I remember, popping up here and there all over the colony, most often where he was least expected. Workers gathering coconuts or weeding in the gardens would see him pass by; convicts in the hospital would open their eyes and find him standing by the bed; men in solitary would glimpse his face peering in at them. He was everywhere, moving silently in long, rapid strides, often alone, always unarmed, carrying only, like a British officer, a riding crop that he would tap nervously against his leg or slap gently into his hand. We called him "the Wheel," because he seemed quite literally to roll from place to place, his eyes flicking quickly about, taking in everything. The speed and unexpectedness of his travels could and did cause frequent dismay in many quarters. A cry of "the Wheel" or "Here comes 'the Wheel'" would send men scrambling in all directions, and his sudden appearance anywhere was likely to be greeted by a peculiar stillness and expressions of childlike innocence on hardbitten faces. And "the Wheel" would roll silently on, not stopping to punish or reprimand, but only observing. He never missed a thing.

One day I happened to be present when a burly guard accosted the commandant during one of his tours. This man had been put in charge of a special work detail made up of convicts whose smoking privileges had been temporarily taken away for some infringement of the rules. The guard had caught the men smoking and had written up a voluminous report on the matter, which he now proudly presented to the commandant. Bonnard barely glanced at it, not even bothering to read it. Instead, he folded up the report, tore it methodically into several pieces, and wordlessly handed it back to the guard. The man was stupefied and stood there, staring at the torn pieces of his report. "You may go," the commandant said quietly.

"But, Chief," the man stammered, "these men are guilty! They were smoking!"

Bonnard looked at him. "They should not have been smoking," he said mildly.

The man still did not understand. He began to insist and Bonnard cut him off. "If you had done your job properly," he said, "they would not have been able to smoke. I cannot punish them without punishing you. You may go."

He was of medium height, thin, with a long, lean face, penetrating eyes, and a firm mouth. He was always elegantly dressed and he moved with the grace of a true aristocrat. You would have said that he was a member in good standing of the Parisian *haut monde*, but in reality he was a man of humble origin, probably from one of the poorer quarters of Paris. His polished manners were self-taught and he was certainly self-educated. Often I would stop by his house in the late afternoons, usually to report on my progress with Paul, and I never failed to find him with a book on his lap. He was a voracious and discriminating reader, of novels as well as technical books, of verse as well as psychological treatises on prison administration. He was at ease in any society and was as respected by his superiors as by the men under his command and jurisdiction. He knew how to punish and he knew how to pardon; he knew when to see and when not to see. He was, in short, the right man.

Being the right man for that job, however, exacted a certain price, a price in human warmth that was paid in great part

by his wife. *Madame* Lise Bonnard was a native of Guiana
and herself the daughter of a prison official. She had met and
married Julien during his early years as a minor functionary
of the camp at St. Laurent and she had known what sort of
life she was in for. But that had not made it any easier on her
and it had not prepared her for the almost inhuman rigidity
of her husband's personal code. To Julien Bonnard discipline
and justice were all that counted and he made no distinctions
in his personal life, not even in his relations with his wife and
children, between his official and private self. He was incapable of unbending and it was said on Royale that his wife was
a *malheureuse*, an unlucky woman.

If there were men on the islands who did not like and feared
Julien, there was no one who did not love his wife. She was
a lovely, soft-spoken, gentle creature with golden hair and
large, expressive eyes. Those of us who were lucky enough to
be working in the area around the commandant's house bene-
fited most from her kindness and we all, even the most hardened villains, would find an excuse to stroll past the garden
where she liked to sit so that we could bask in her smile. She
would often ask us to stop a moment and perform some small
task for her, and she never failed to reward us with a glass
of rum, a bite to eat, or a few francs with which we could buy
tobacco. Of course this was against the rules and Julien was
well aware of his wife's activities, but in this case he made
a supreme effort and looked the other way, though it must have
caused him some discomfort. He was all head and logic and
she was merely a human being. Perhaps the only quality they
had in common was a sense of humor.

One day, toward the end of Julien Bonnard's second year
on Royale, I was high on a ladder, putting the finishing touches
to one of my murals in the church, when I heard my name

called. I looked down and saw *Madame* Lise standing in a side
entrance. "Lagrange," she said, "I need your help." I climbed
down and followed her back to the house, which was only a
few minutes' walk from the church.

When we got there, *Madame* Lise led me around to the
back where there was a small chicken coop. She pointed out
a large, tough-looking rooster. The bird evidently knew what
was up because he was pacing nervously along the fence, peering at us out of a small, wicked eye. "That rooster," *Madame*
Lise said apologetically, "I've been trying to catch him all
morning."

"That's easy, *Madame*," I said. "I'll catch him for you."
Smiling confidently, I entered the coop and started for the bird.

It was a merry chase. The old rooster had mastered every
trick handed down by generations of desperate chickens. Finally, after what seemed hours of fruitless pursuit, I managed
to corner the creature and I flung myself on it with a triumphant cry. Holding it tightly in my arms, I picked myself up
and faced *Madame* Lise, who was having difficulty trying to
keep a straight face. Sweaty, caked with dust, I beamed at
her. "There you are, *Madame!*" I said. "Where would you like
me to put him?"

At that very moment, the bird gave me a vicious peck and
relieved himself all over my shirt. "Look! Look!" I shrieked,
nearly beside myself with rage. "Look what he's done!"

Madame Lise laughed merrily and put a comforting hand
on my shoulder. "But my dear Lagrange," she said, "it's only
merde! You can easily wash it off!"

I remember this trivial anecdote about *Madame* Lise and
the rooster because it was on the very next day that I saw her
for the last time. I had left the church at midday and was on
my way back to my cell block when I passed her on the road

leading up to the hospital. She was alone and carrying a small sack under her arm. She looked a little pale, but I thought nothing of it at the time.

"Well, *Madame*," I said cheerfully, "how goes it?"

"Not well at all," she answered. "I'm ill. I'm going to the hospital." I must have looked stunned because she made an effort to smile and said: "Perhaps it is nothing, Lagrange. I haven't even told Julien. They will fetch him if I must stay there."

Twenty-four hours later she was dead.

Unknown to any of us, she had suffered for years from heart disease. But she had always minimized her illness, so that not even her husband had been aware of the extent of it.

On the day of her death I had gone up to the hospital to see her, but Julien had preceded me and I stood in the corridor outside her room, waiting for him to leave. The door had been left slightly ajar and I was able to overhear part of their conversation. *Madame* Lise's voice sounded alarmingly weak. "Julien," she said, "don't send me to St. Joseph. I want to sleep here, among the children."

I couldn't believe my ears; she was referring to her burial. The main cemetery for the deceased of the administration is on St. Joseph, while on Royale there is only a small plot of ground behind the church where lie the graves of the few children who have died on the islands. I was badly shaken, but I still couldn't imagine that *Madame* Lise was so desperately ill.

"Don't be stupid, Lise," her husband answered coldly. "You're not going to die. Don't talk rot!"

"But——"

"And besides, it's against the rules!"

I could barely hear her now, her voice had grown so faint,

but I could imagine her large, understanding eyes fixed calmly on her husband as she answered. "Ah, yes, Julien," she said, "the rules!"

"Lise, you are *not* going to die!"

"But if I should," she continued, "if I should, Julien, I want you to promise. . . ."

"Don't be stupid, Lise!"

"Please, Julien . . . promise. . . ."

There was a pause and then at last he spoke. His voice was strangely altered, gruff, but it was always under control. There was no room for tears in Julien Bonnard's world. "All right," he said, "I promise. I'll arrange it. But it's all a lot of rot. You're not going to die."

I did not hear any more. I suddenly *knew* that *Madame* Lise was going to die and I could not remain and face that. I walked out of the hospital as quickly as I could.

She died that evening and a telegram was sent to Cayenne requesting permission to bury her in the children's cemetery on Royale. The next morning permission was granted and that afternoon *Madame* Lise was laid to rest among her children. There was not a man on the island who did not mourn her.

A few weeks later, Julien Bonnard took his sons back to France. With the death of his wife and his departure, an era ended for all of us in the *bagne*.

4 *The Best Intentions*

WHAT led me to the *bagne* in the first place? Perhaps it was because I began life with the very best intentions, which, as everyone knows, is the fastest way to get to hell. I don't mean to imply that I was a model son and always motivated by the noblest ideals. I was too prone to take short cuts, too eager to smack my lips over life's tasty morsels and gorge myself on them. I was almost always in trouble with authorities of all kinds because I could never imagine living or wanting to live according to rules. By the best intentions I mean that I believed in living fully, in not harming anyone, in accepting everything, both good and bad, that life would have to offer. It is not an attitude that most people understand or tolerate very willingly. It has nothing to do with social morality. It has been my lifelong inability to grasp this central fact of life that has brought about most of my difficulties. It is only logical, I suppose, that I should have wound up in prison.

I must have been the despair of my parents. They were both solid bourgeois types. Not dull, but hard-working and dedicated to proceeding along familiar ruts. I was an only child, high-spirited, full of mischief, a large nuisance. We traveled a good deal, which was fine for me in some ways (I learned to speak other languages, for instance) and bad in others. My education was acquired in odd chunks—a month here, two weeks there, a year in another place, and then another uprooting. I was a brilliant student in any subject that interested me (languages, history, art, music), dismal in all others. My mother used to cluck over me and worry and complain that I was never in any one place long enough to become civilized, but there was no help for it. My father's job required him to travel constantly and he preferred not to be absent from my mother for months at a time. I'm sure he was right to feel that way and I can't believe that our nomad existence really contributed in any significant manner to my career in crime. In another decade, in some other place, I might have lived and died a lawful if unrespected citizen. I would never have been the pillar of any community, but the line between respectability and the twilight world of chicanery is thin, almost invisible, and people cross it, back and forth, every day.

My father was an engraver and art restorer, one of the best in Europe, and he was naturally in much demand. Private collectors and museums paid well for his services, since his skill was used to preserve and restore the masterpieces of the past. He had begun as a painter, but he had not been gifted with the imagination and creative drive of the real artist. He had found his true career in restoration, work in which his individuality was submerged in another's and only his technical ability counted. I was fascinated by his work and he fondly believed that I would follow in his wake. He taught me all his skills, poor man, though fortunately he did not live long enough to find out how I used them.

My mother was Scottish. She was a slender, silent woman, affectionate enough but not outgoing. She was subject to long bouts of melancholy and would periodically flee back to her beloved Highlands, where something in the cold air of those open spaces appealed irresistibly to her. Sometimes she took me with her, but I did not share her enthusiasm for damp mountain slopes and mile after mile of forbidding heather. I was my father's child in that respect. I had a Parisian's love of companionship; I wanted people and warmth around me.

I discovered quite early in life that the most desirable people were women and that the most delicious kind of warmth was to be found in their arms. I made this notable discovery at the age of fifteen with the wholehearted co-operation of the daughter of one of my father's English clients. She was several years older than I and experienced in a number of delightful ways. Unfortunately, my father discovered us one afternoon clasped in each other's arms behind a tapestry. Not too many words were exchanged, but our departure from the client's household was hurried.

My father did his best to reform me. I politely listened to a series of long lectures on the dangers of sexual impropriety, but I was never able to take them seriously. Unlike that tedious moralist Lord Chesterfield, I was fully prepared to take all the risks, undergo all the hardships, put up with all the consequences merely to taste one fleeting moment of rapture. I embraced the spirit of Don Juan and stalked Europe in quest of prey. I've never had much in the way of looks, but something in me has always appealed to women. Great big lovely girls would steal one glance at my thin, wiry frame and foxy little face and they would open their arms to me. I was so successful that I began to develop a small reputation. My father tried sterner measures. When they failed, he lost several clients. Our travels became more frenzied, our departures hastier. I had found myself a career at last.

Unfortunately for me, I soon started to fall in love with my victims. I became the star actor in a number of tender, tearful farewell scenes. My inability to remain a cold-blooded seducer beyond the age of seventeen was to cost me dearly later. I was always in love, always the fool. I never failed to believe the best of all my flirts and I was almost always disappointed in the end. Women, I may say right here, have been the great joy of my life, though my total dedication to them has invariably been repaid by disaster. I never learned. I'm as big a fool today as I was then, though not quite so vulnerable.

When I was about twenty, my father gave up on me. It was either that or the abandonment of his life's work. Too many of his clients had daughters, cousins, nieces, and wives. To defend his income and preserve his sanity he dispatched my mother and me to Hamburg, where I continued my studies during the day and my amatory career at night. We had picked Hamburg because we had been there before and had friends in the city and because I already spoke excellent German. Also, as one of the few resident Frenchmen, I was much in demand. I don't know whether the French really deserve their international reputation in matters of the heart, but I do know that that reputation exists and that it behooves every able-bodied citizen of France to defend the national honor by living up to it. I did my best, which I think was quite adequate.

I was extremely happy in Hamburg. In addition to my usual curricular and extracurricular activities, I began to paint on my own. For hours at a time I would manage to forget about women. I toured the galleries and museums, attended all the openings, and joined a happy beer-drinking group of Bohemians, all of whom were as dedicated as I to all the underground virtues and equally indifferent to all the accepted social codes.

We thought of ourselves as very daring and very swashbuck-
ling. I also earned some extra money in restoration for several wealthy private collectors and by working a few hours a
week in a large printing and engraving establishment. I was
laying a very firm groundwork for my future career, though,
of course, I had no idea then of the peculiar twists of fate in
store for me.

We lived in Hamburg for nearly a year and I had begun to
think of myself as a native of the city. I was living a full, rich
life and I was quite oblivious of the outside world. That world,
of course, was crumbling, but I was too young, too self-
engrossed to see it. The first real hint I had of it was in an
urgent letter from my father. He had returned to Paris and
was supposed to have come and stayed with us for a few weeks
before going back to England and another museum job. In his
letter he predicted the outbreak of war and said that he was
afraid to come. I was to pack everything and return to Paris
with Mother at once. It was 1914. I was just twenty-one
years old and my world had suddenly been turned upside
down for the first time.

The evidence was all around me, in the very air we
breathed, but I wouldn't acknowledge it. I almost convinced
myself that everything was simply splendid. I shut my eyes
to the sight of uniforms and my ears to the sound of marching
feet. When a few of my German friends began to stare at me
with hostile eyes, I shrugged it off. My mother began to pack,
but I laughed at her. I was willing to concede that there was
a certain amount of tension in the air, but I assured her that
it would soon blow away. Wouldn't we look foolish when it
did? The whole thing was absurd and I would have nothing
to do with it. My mother gave up and prepared to leave without me.

I couldn't bear to face reality because, as usual, I was in love. The girl's name was Maria Bauer. She was two years younger than I, a dark-haired beauty with dimples, rosy cheeks, a tiny waist, deep-set black eyes, and a smile that could melt stones. She couldn't believe in the war either. We must have been the only two people in Hamburg who didn't.

On the morning of my mother's scheduled departure, one of my Bohemian cronies came to see me. His name was Franz. He was a tall, thin boy with wispy blond hair, eyes set very close together over an enormous beak of a nose, and he had an absolutely inexhaustible supply of bawdy jokes. On this particular morning he wasn't joking. He stood in our living room, looking very tall and stiff, staring at us with alarmed, unblinking eyes. "You must leave Hamburg at once," he said, "or you will be arrested."

I thought he was mad and told him so. My mother began to cry and rushed out of the room. Franz took me by the arm. "Don't be an idiot, Flag," he said urgently. "There's going to be a war and when it starts everyone will remember that you are French and so an enemy. Already they are remembering. They will arrest you. You must leave today."

I sat down rather heavily. I suddenly knew that Franz was right. "I want to say good-by to Maria," I said.

"Impossible," Franz told me. "Her family has taken her away to the country. They knew they couldn't keep you apart if she were in the city, so late last night they took her out. One of the gang came by and told me. The Bauers don't like you anyway, you know that, and now the war has given them the excuse they needed. I also heard that one of them was planning to denounce you as a French spy."

I must have been the picture of outraged astonishment because Franz, worried as he was, could not resist a smile. "Me?" I said. "A spy?"

Franz nodded heavily. "You must go, Flag. Someday this idiocy will be over and you will come back to us, but now you must go. I'll find a way to say good-by to her for you."

I rushed to my desk and scribbled Maria a note. Franz put it in his pocket and we threw our arms around each other, promising to remain friends and to look each other up after the war. Then, without another word, he turned and walked out. That night my mother and I left Hamburg. When I finally did come back after the war, I learned that Franz had been killed during the first year of the campaign on the western front.

As it happened, we left in the nick of time, crossing over the border just as hostilities were being declared, and rejoined Father in Paris, where everything was in a state of almost total confusion. Everyone felt terribly patriotic and no one thought the war would last more than a few months. We would simply sweep the Germans away and, along with our British and Russian allies, crush them forever. My father was more pessimistic than most—he thought it might take as long as a year to settle everything—but he was equally certain of a swift and total victory. Also, he was particularly bitter in his denunciations of Germany and Germans as a whole. Who could blame him? The war had made us suddenly poor, since it was no longer possible to travel freely and the calls for my father's services became few and far between. It was all the fault of the dirty *Boches!*

The year in Hamburg had been the happiest of my life. I couldn't bring myself to hate Germans and I refused to concede that the war was entirely their fault. This liberal attitude struck my father as treasonable and we began to argue all day

long. I tried to remind him of all the friends he himself had
made in Germany, but he refused to listen to me. He had
never had any friends in Germany, he said, only clients! Germany was a pigsty and the Germans were a race of pigs! They
would be mercilessly wiped out and the world would be rid
of them forever!

At first my mother remained neutral and tried to make peace
between us, but inevitably she began to side more and more
with my father. She was above all other things an obedient
wife. I was above all other things an ungrateful son; I persisted in thinking for myself and in denying that any one race
of human beings could be held accountable for all the evil in
the world. Conversations with my father became increasingly
acrimonious. On the day I announced that I intended to return to Hamburg after the war and marry Maria Bauer, my
father stopped speaking to me.

Despite my troubles at home and my fond memories of
Hamburg days, however, I did not forget that I was French.
I think, perhaps, I have made it clear that I am no super-
patriot. If one is to live a civilized life, how is it possible to
swallow slogans and march with the mob? I am nothing if not
a civilized man. But it is possible to remain civilized and in-
dependent-minded and still love one's country. I knew that,
if the war lasted, I could not stay aloof from it. When it not
only became clear that the war would last but that the Germans might very well win it, I went down to the nearest re-
cruiting station and enlisted. For two days I didn't tell my
parents about it. When they found out, my mother cried and
my father gazed at me triumphantly. "No," I said to him, "I
still don't believe the Germans are merely beasts. And I still
intend to return there after the war. I enlisted because I am

a man and there was nothing else I could do. I'm sorry for all of us involved in this mess."

My father didn't answer me. On the day I went into the service, he didn't even say good-by to me. If I had kept quiet when I should have and allowed him to be proud of me, perhaps the breach between us would have been healed. But it would have meant denying everything in life of any importance to me and I was unable to do that. I did not know it then, but when I left the house that day it was to be the last time I was ever under my father's roof.

5 Respectability

MY war years were undistinguished and dull, so there's not much use dwelling on them at any length. I had wanted to go into aviation because the whole idea appealed to my romantic nature, but I was assigned to Intelligence instead. This had sounded exciting enough (I had expected some glamorous assignment, perhaps a personal duel of wit and charm with Mata Hari herself), but my job turned out to be a routine business. Because of my fluent German, I was used mostly as an interpreter and translator. I spent the war in an office, feeling comfortably safe but bored. Like everyone else, I waited for the war to end and fumed as the years dragged by.

When at last it was over and I found myself back in Paris, trying to reassemble the fabric of my life, I began to devote my energies to returning to Hamburg. This was not as easy as one might think. Jobs were scarce, I could not ask my father for help, and I wasn't even certain what I would find in Hamburg if I did manage to get there. Nevertheless, I was determined. I was going to recapture all the freedom and joy of those last months before the world went mad. Most important, I was going to find Maria Bauer.

Finally, after several months of floundering about and one last bitter scene with my father, I hit on a solution. I had heard from a wartime colleague of mine that the Intelligence Service was ready to finance civilian informers in Germany as well as in other nations. As an ex-member of the Service, I would certainly receive priority and, since Hamburg was such an important port and naval base, the chances of my being able to operate there would be good. I rushed at once to the Ministry of War and presented myself.

The whole affair was arranged in less than a week. I was to file a regular tri-monthly report and to be available for any special assignments my French contacts would give me. For this I was to be paid a small yearly retainer, no fortune but enough to live on decently in those postwar depression years. The reports were not especially complicated, to judge by the samples I was shown. They were simply long, detailed analyses of political, economic, and military developments and their possible influence on French affairs. I anticipated no difficulty in writing them. I was to bring them to the French consulate in Hamburg and I was told that they were to be taken back to France by diplomatic mail pouch. Germany had lost the war, but evidently she was still regarded as a potentially dangerous enemy and had to be watched. I considered the business merely an extension of wartime imbecility, but I kept this opinion to myself. If someone wanted to pay me enough money to return me to the one place I wanted to go, I was quite willing to participate in any amount of foolishness. I kept a straight face, promised to be a good spy, swore allegiance to God and country again, and went home to pack. The next day I was on my way back to my beloved Hamburg.

Of course things were not the same and it took some time to adjust to what I found. Many of my old roistering companions had been killed or wounded and the atmosphere of the place was different. There was an air of bitterness and desolation in the once prosperous streets; poverty gripped the city in a cold, iron fist. Being French had become something of a liability and I did not emphasize my national status. Hamburg, like the rest of Europe, had changed a great deal, and not for the better. Nevertheless, I was immensely happy to be back. I rented myself a small studio, set up my easel, sought out old friends, and began to inquire after Maria.

The Bauers, it turned out, had done very well for themselves during the war. They were a large, tightly knit family of the upper bourgeoisie, well-connected, self-interested, and opportunistic, the sort of people who seem to survive all national catastrophes, always bobbing to the surface of society sleeker and fatter than ever. Regimes come and go, but the Bauers of the world sit tight and grow richer and richer. *Herr* Bauer, Maria's father, had made himself a tidy wartime fortune in textiles; General Bauer, his older brother, had led his regiments to a series of Pyrrhic victories on the Russian front and had been retired with honors; Uncle Hans Bauer, the younger brother, had enriched himself exchanging currencies through Switzerland and had emerged from the war as a financial leader. All of the Bauer wives had grown a little stout and shrill and were nearly invisible under their new furs. In fact, the Bauers and their friends were the very people George Grosz would caricature so viciously in his paintings and drawings of postwar Germany. And need it be added that the family would doubtless be among the first to support Hitler? In any case, they were then living in a large house in one of the richest residential suburbs of the city and they were not at all glad to see me. Except for Maria.

She had not forgotten me, probably because, surrounded as

she was by such relatives, I must have seemed like a man from another planet to her. She was the exception that proved the rule about the Bauers, in personality as well as in appearance. She was introspective, sensitive, and shy, qualities unknown to the rest of her family. We had met at a gallery opening a few weeks before I was forced to leave Germany and had fallen immediately in love. She appealed to everything that was most masculine and protective in me and to her I represented freedom, culture, the artistic, unconventional life, something attractive and strong enough to pull her away from the dull materialism of her home. When we met again on her doorstep five years later, we fell in love more deeply than before and this time, because she was no longer a minor, not even her family's objections could keep us apart.

Despite my very genuine affection for Maria, I confess that I probably wouldn't have married her if it hadn't been for her family. I knew instinctively that I was not the sort of man who ought to get married. I could be faithful to a woman, yes, and I could love, but I could not live the quiet, respectable life for very long. Under ordinary circumstances, my love affair with Maria would probably have run the usual course—rapture, irritations, open quarrels, reconciliations, more quarrels, the tender farewell scene—but the frenzied opposition of her family aroused me to fury. They did everything they could to force us apart. Once, the ancient general even paid me a visit and brandished a cane about my studio, threatening me with a public beating if I persisted in my attentions to his niece. *Herr* Bauer had me followed by detectives. Ugly letters arrived in my mailbox. Maria herself was threatened with disinheritance. What could I do? I would show them, I would teach them a lesson. I married her.

However, after she had moved into my studio, I began to

surprise myself. I became a model husband: I worked hard, remained faithful, gave up two or three of my more disreputable friends, and tried to heal the breach with her relatives. After a year or so, her parents consented to see her, but they never acknowledged my existence. I was careful not to slip. I knew that her family was waiting patiently, hopefully for the day when my real character would assert itself and they would have to rescue Maria from the pit into which she had fallen. For the first and only time in my life I became the simple bourgeois. Maria was very happy and, strangely, so was I.

Though I led a comparatively humdrum life, I don't mean to imply that I abandoned my old ways entirely. I still met my cronies at the café, still spent hours arguing deep topics with them well into the night, still occasionally passed an evening carousing with them through the town. And, of course, I continued to paint. During our second year together, I had my first show. I was working along Impressionist lines in those days (I suppose you could say I am still an Impressionist, though I hate to feel labeled) and my work aroused favorable critical comments. I even sold several paintings, which helped to ease some of the financial pressure on us, since, needless to say, we were receiving no help from the Bauers. It didn't matter. Nothing mattered to us except our life together and my work. I was painting, I was earning some money in a printing establishment, and I was in love. It was more than enough.

Four years passed in this manner. Maria gave birth to twin girls and we moved into a larger studio. I had a second show and sold more paintings. The Bauers persisted in their efforts to ruin the marriage. I watched my step, remained faithful to Maria, managed not to see too much of my friends, and told myself that I was a truly lucky man; I had a loving wife, ador-

able daughters, loyal friends, and success in my work. I saw
the whole pattern of my life laid out for me, but, though it
saddened me to think the future would no longer hold any
surprises, I was contentedly resigned to it. I could not imagine
any other life for myself.

Then, one day, as I was strolling through downtown Hamburg, a dark, round-faced man took me by the arm. "Flag!"
he said in French. "Aren't you Francis Lagrange? You don't
know me?"

I looked at him for a moment, my mind a blank, then I
remembered. The man's name was Cellier; he had been
a colleague of mine in the Intelligence Service during the war.
In the light of later events, I should have been puzzled by his
evident delight at seeing me, since we had never been close
friends. But at the time it seemed only natural. He told me
that he was now an officer in the merchant marine, that his
ship had docked that day in the harbor, and that he had a
few hours to kill. I invited him to kill them with us and took
him home to meet Maria.

In the usual manner of reunions, we spent the afternoon
and evening reminiscing. By the time dinner had been served,
I had remembered not liking Cellier. There had always
been something secretive, something shifty-eyed about him. I
thought nothing more of it. He now seemed affable enough
and I enjoyed talking to him. He was the only Frenchman I
had talked to since returning to Germany.

Later, after Maria had excused herself and gone to bed,
Cellier looked at me slyly and gave me a knowing wink.
"Well, Flag," he said, "and what about your present job?"

"My present job?"

"Oh, you know," he continued, gesturing airily, "your assignment, the reports."

"The reports? What reports?"

Cellier's smile became a bit forced and he leaned forward across the table between us. He knew all about the reports, he whispered, the ones I was sending in regularly to headquarters through the consular mail pouch. He was himself still working for the Intelligence Service, he said, on a sort of roving assignment basis. I had been one of the contacts given him in Paris.

I stared at him, then I laughed. "My God," I said, "I had forgotten all about that!"

It was true; I *had* forgotten all about it. Since my return to Hamburg, I had sent exactly one report back to Paris and it had contained nothing but information I had culled from the newspapers. After that, silence. I had stopped sending reports, Paris had stopped sending me money, and no one had ever tried to contact me about it. The whole idea had struck me from the first as an absurdity and I had made use of the arrangement simply to get back to Germany. Once I had established myself and was making enough money on my own, I could see no reason to continue my part in such ridiculous proceedings.

I explained all this to Cellier and he looked at me strangely. "You mean to say that all this time they think you are a spy in Paris and you don't send in any reports?" he asked.

"I guess that's right," I said. "Isn't it absurd?"

Cellier and I had a good laugh over it. After a few more minutes, he stood up, shook my hand, and left. I thought nothing more of it and went to bed that night with only the usual cares of a happy family man on my mind.

Three days later, early in the morning, I was arrested and taken to police headquarters for interrogation. The man who interviewed me was in civilian clothes. He was short and fat, with a heavy pink face and hysterical eyes. He sat behind a desk and shuffled methodically through a sheaf of papers while I stood in front of him. I still had no idea why I had been arrested and I was indignant. The man allowed me to ramble on for a few minutes, then slammed his hand down on the desk. "Shut up, you dirty spy!" he bellowed. "How dare you play the innocent with me?"

I gaped at him, unable to grasp at first what he meant. Me a spy? It was all some sort of hideous practical joke. How could anyone think— At last I understood: Cellier. Somehow someone had found out about my old status with the French Intelligence Service and sicked an informer on me. Dear old Cellier!

I tried to make light of the situation. I smiled and started to explain. The interrogator shouted me down. "Do you know what we do with spies in Germany?" he said. "We hang them! Or we put them up against a wall and shoot them! That's what we do with spies in Germany, you filthy, lousy French dog!"

It was a very curious interrogation. I kept my balance and repeatedly tried to explain, but the man refused to listen. He stormed up and down the room, kicking at the walls, pounding his fists on the desk, rushing to put his face up to mine and shout threats at me. Finally, I just gave up and waited for him to run down. It took some time, but at last I was able to speak. "I have nothing to say," I told him quietly, "until I can consult my lawyer."

That set him off again. "Your lawyer? Your lawyer?" he screamed. "Dirty French spies don't have lawyers! Dirty French spies don't have rights!" There was a good deal more of this sort of thing, after which the man rang a bell and I was taken off to a cell.

For two weeks I sat in this cell, helpless, unable to communicate with anyone on the outside. Twice a day, morning and evening, I was taken back to the office where the interrogator pounded his desk, kicked at the walls, and continued to scream insults at me. I was never able to explain. Every time I said something, the interrogator would resume his pounding and kicking and abuse. I was to be shot, I was to be hanged, I was to be torn apart by savage animals. I was scum. I was a swine. I was a dirty French this and a dirty French that. I would get what I deserved, all right. He, the interrogator, would see to that, all right. My fingernails would be torn out. Water would drip on my head. Whips would flay me alive. I was a curse and an obscenity.

I gave up. I began to believe that the real German method of punishing spies was to put them in a room with a madman twice a day. It was a punishment, I thought, quite worthy of a subtle police intelligence. What torture is more atrocious than the inability to communicate with a single other human being?

Then, late one night, I was taken out of my cell and into another, smaller office. A man with a dull-gray face, who was dressed in a food-stained police uniform, was waiting for me. Silently, without even looking at me, he handed me my passport and the other personal belongings which had been taken from me on the morning of my arrest. "I'm free?" I asked.

The man still refused to look at me. He yawned and stared at the wall. "You will be escorted to the French border and turned over to the French authorities," he said in a colorless, mechanical voice.

"When?"

"Tonight."

"But my family——"

"You will see no one and communicate with no one before

leaving," the man said. "You will not return to Germany again. If you do, you will be arrested and it will not be so easy on you next time." He said all this as if he were reading a weather report or a railroad timetable. Again I tried to explain, but this one, in his own colorless way, was as unreachable as my interrogator. "I have my orders," was all he said. "I do what I am told."

An hour later I was on my way out of Germany. By the afternoon of the following day I was back in Paris, alone, nearly penniless, stripped of everything I owned. I at once tried to telephone Maria. She was not home. I finally located her at her parents' house. They would not let me speak to her. I was a dirty spy, they had known it all along, she was well rid of me. If I returned to Germany, they would know what to do with me. They hung up.

I dropped the telephone receiver and walked out into the streets of my native city. It was a cold, gray day, with a wind whistling along the boulevards. People hurried past me, heads down, coats buttoned up against the cold. I was absolutely alone in all the world. For the second time in my young life, the universe had capriciously dumped me on my head. I never saw or heard from Maria again. Many years later, after my release from prison, I got indirect word of her from an old ex-convict friend of mine who had passed through Hamburg and tried to look her up for me. He told me that she and the children, then young women in their teens, had been killed during the air bombardments of World War II.

6 Enter Ludwig van Beethoven

ANOTHER man might have mourned the rest of his life. Fortunately for my peace of mind, I am not made that way. I can't pretend that I was happy at losing everything, but I adjusted. At first I told myself that someday, somehow I would find Maria and the children again; I would return to Germany and resume where I had left off. However, at heart I knew that I was lying to myself and I had enough strength of character not to take the lie too seriously.

I had not been cut out for respectability and eventually Maria, whose bourgeois instincts were too strong to be permanently overcome, would have left me and returned to her monstrous family. After all, she had been quick enough to do so at the very first crisis; she had refused to wait for a possible explanation and I couldn't believe that even her family could have prevented her from seeing me or talking to me or making some effort to contact me. If I never heard from her again, it was because both of us must have instinctively realized that we had reached the end of a road that had nothing to do with my arrest and expulsion from Hamburg. A disastrous misunderstanding had parted us, but surely at the right time. I wept some genuine tears over my loss and immediately plunged into my new environment, like a fish transferred from one aquarium to another. Life, after all, is too important not to be lived.

However, the water was very cold in Paris that winter of 1925–26. No matter how fast I swam or in what direction, I couldn't seem to get warm. I was thirty-two, full of juice, proud of my ability to land always on my feet, but this was unquestionably the most desperate period of my life. It was so desperate that I even made an attempt to throw myself temporarily upon the mercy of my long-forgotten parents. I showed up one afternoon at the front door of the apartment house I believed they might be living in. In any case, it was the last address I had had for them. When I couldn't find their names on the list of tenants, I presented myself to the janitress. "I am searching for *Monsieur* and *Madame* Lagrange," I told her. "I believe they used to live here."

The janitress gazed at me blankly. She was a stout, slovenly, middle-aged woman with a face like a decaying pudding. I thought that her silence was due to my suspiciously destitute appearance—I could have stepped right into the first act of *La Bohème*—and I hastened to reassure her. "I am their son," I said.

The blank expression on the creature's face changed to one of utter astonishment. "Their son?" she said, mouth agape to reveal an uneven row of small, gray teeth embedded in purple gums. "You are the son?"

I had been having a good deal to do recently with lunatics and idiots, so I was quite prepared to cope with another cretin. I smiled and explained that I had been out of the country for some time and had mislaid their address. Could *Madame* give me some indication of their present whereabouts?

Apparently, I had made no impression; the creature continued to regard me with incredulity. "You are the son," she said, "and you do not know?"

"Know what?"

The woman's jaw sagged another inch. She really had an unbearable mouth. "You do not know that your parents died last spring?"

Now it was my turn to play the cretin. We stood there and regarded each other, a couple of blind morons suddenly endowed with sight and set face to face. "Died?" I stammered.

The woman nodded. *Monsieur* Lagrange had been suddenly stricken, she said, influenza it was, and taken to the hospital. He had died in a few days. Then *Madame* Lagrange had been stricken in her turn and taken to the hospital. She, too, had died in a few days. How was it that no one had informed me? Where had I been? That had happened months ago. It had been quite an elaborate funeral, with the whole neighborhood present. No one knew there had been a son. If someone had known, surely *Monsieur* would have been informed. Perhaps. . . .

Dazed, I turned and left her babbling to herself. What else was going to happen to me that year, I wondered? I went home, shed a few more tears, and drank far too much for several days. After I recovered, I took careful stock. Evidently, I was going to have to concentrate simply on keeping myself alive in a world that had become suddenly, inexplicably hostile.

With the last of my money I moved out of the small hotel I had been living in since my arrival in Paris and rented myself a tiny studio on the Left Bank. I picked up a secondhand easel from a junk shop, sold my overcoat to buy brushes and paints, borrowed some canvas from a dealer on the promise that I would execute a naughty painting for a lascivious client of his, and I resumed my career as an artist. After all, I rea-

Below decks the guards patrolled their private zoo.

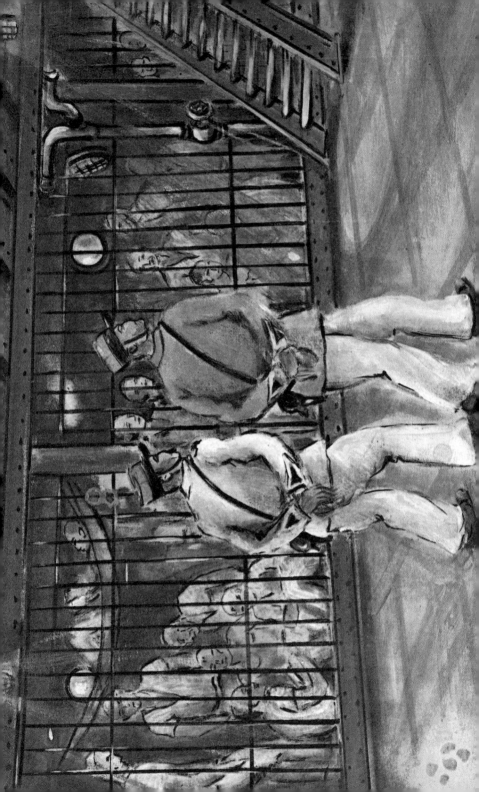

soned, I had been able to support myself very well in Hamburg with my painting; why should Paris be any different? I began to make the rounds of the galleries, to frequent the right cafés, to make the right friends. I waited for the great Parisian art world to sit up and take note of this talented new arrival. The money will roll in, I told myself, if I can only hold on long enough and keep painting.

Paris, I soon learned, is not Hamburg. There are more painters in Paris than people. Absolutely no one took note of me and the money merely trickled in, a few francs at a time. Nor did it trickle in because anyone bought my serious work. I managed to stay alive because my dealer's lascivious client had, it turned out, an insatiable appetite for smut. So I painted masterpieces in the morning, I illustrated the novels of De Sade in the afternoon. I told myself that eventually things would break for me, that soon, any day now, people would realize that a genius was starving and working in their midst. Someone would recognize my talent, would rent a gallery and give me a showing, a showing that would set all Paris on its ear. I was Francis Lagrange, undiscovered genius, soon to be the toast of international art circles. All I had to do was hang on.

I hung on, painting furiously, through the worst winter of my life. I painted and painted, even on the days when the wind hissed through the cracked panes of my skylight and my fingers turned blue. A pile of finished, unbought canvases rose toward the ceiling of my garret; a stream of naughty pictures flowed out through the grimy hands of my dealer. The spring finally came, nothing had changed, and I began to think there was no end to it.

I minded the lack of money even more than the lack of recognition. I have always been able to do without fame, but

The arrival in St. Laurent.

never without money. I was willing to starve for my art, but
not forever. I was used to having money, reasonable amounts
of it, and I was not prepared to give up this deplorable habit.
Of course, it has always been argued that an artist, a real
artist, doesn't think about money; he concentrates ferociously
on his art and allows the money question to take care of itself.

There's no need to engage in a full-scale debate on the matter. I do know that artists have stomachs like other people and
they enjoy filling them as much as anyone else. I don't consider myself any different. That winter in Paris confirmed me
in a growing, now entrenched belief that the absence of
money is the only unforgivable sin (unforgivable because it
can be so easily remedied: any fool can make it, some figuratively, some literally!) and I was sinning that winter in a way
I have managed to avoid ever since. I felt the lack of money
so keenly not only because I needed some for myself but because I was, as usual, embroiled with a woman.

Her name was Paulette and she was as different as could
be from Maria. My placid years were behind me and Paulette
was the future. A high-strung, nervous, flirtatious *midinette*
from the heart of Paris, she played a beautiful Musetta to my
Marcello. We were always quarreling—long, loud arguments
accompanied by the smashing of crockery, the crashing of
furniture—and making up in bed. There were brief, deliriously
happy periods and weeks of sullen misery during which we
hated each other. Paulette loved me, but she also loved the
warmth of cafés and expensive restaurants, the glow of bright
night life, the caress of furs against her cheek, the feel of satin
and silk on her skin. She didn't mind my being an artist, but
she minded terribly my inability to make it pay.

During the summer, things improved. Poverty weighed less
heavily upon us and the long, hot nights in each other's arms

compensated for the weeks of bitter cold, the inadequate food, the absence of all the small and large luxuries that cushion life. My work was still going badly—I had not managed to sell even one of my masterpieces—but under a warm August sun it did not seem to matter so much. Paris itself became a feast and we gorged ourselves upon it. But I knew that with the first nip of fall, the first breath of cold wind across the city, all that would end. I was sure Paulette would leave me and I would be alone again. With sinking heart, I counted the days.

The first quarrel of the cold season had hardly been settled in the usual ecstatic way when my doorbell rang. I put on a bathrobe and stumbled to the door. It was the postman with a registered letter from Switzerland. When I opened it, I found myself holding a check for 500 francs and a congratulatory letter stating that I had won second prize in the Beethoven Centennary Competition.

It was a minute or two before I grasped what had happened. Early that spring I had seen in a newspaper the announcement of a Swiss competition for the design of a new postage stamp to commemorate the one hundredth anniversary of the death of Ludwig van Beethoven in 1827. The winning design was to be rewarded with a prize of 1000 francs and used for the new stamp, and there were second, third, and fourth prizes as well. I had entered the competition with a drawing of the deaf, aging composer seated at his keyboard, mailed the design to Geneva, and forgotten all about it. I had not heard a word until that very moment.

I dropped the letter on the floor and began to waltz wildly about the room. Paulette sat up in bed and stared at me. I danced up to her and waved the check under her nose. "Get up, get up, you silly beast!" I shouted. "We're rich! We're going out! We're going to dine in style!"

Five hundred francs was a not inconsiderable sum in those days. It should have supported us through at least part of the winter, if we had been prudent and spent every sou on necessities. I am happy to say that Paulette and I went through the money in less than twenty-four hours. And, needless to add, we went through it with a flourish. Money, I have always felt, is too enjoyable to be spent wisely.

We should have been punished, made to suffer for our extravagance. We should not, by all the accepted standards, have been allowed to enjoy ourselves so irresponsibly and escape retribution. But the truth of the matter is that from this moment our fortunes began to improve. The very morning that we again woke up penniless, with nothing in view, a friend stopped by and told me that I was wanted by the impresario of a small music hall. He had seen some of my sketches and would commission me to design the sets for his new musical revue. Paulette and I embraced, and the future turned beautifully rosy.

The musical revue opened and closed. Paulette bought herself hats and dresses and a small necklace of cultured pearls. I bought a suit, some ties, a dozen bottles of good champagne, and yards of canvas. We spent the last few francs on a good meal. Then we went back to the garret, settled in bed, surrounded by champagne bottles, and waited. Neither of us had the slightest doubt that fate had taken a hand; our luck had turned and all we had to do now was wait for the doorbell to ring again.

It did, about a week later. When I went to open it—in my bathrobe, of course—a small, dapper gentleman in a dark suit was standing in the hallway. He had a smooth, round face, vaguely Oriental in appearance, with straight, black hair parted down the middle and a small Chaplinesque mustache.

When he smiled, he displayed two perfectly matched rows of bright, hard little teeth. I took him at once for a man of the theater and invited him in.

He bowed, entered, and stood looking about my dingy studio with visible distaste. I indicated a battered armchair and he lowered himself into it like a man entering a tub full of scalding water. Paulette had gone out. I sat down on the edge of the bed and prepared to negotiate. If this was to be another musical revue, I was going to demand considerably more money. I plotted sums in my head.

The little man finally broke the silence. "I will come right to the point," he said. He spoke precise faintly accented French in a small, rather sweet tenor voice. "You do not wish to remain poor?"

I shook my head and continued to calculate feverishly.

The little man smiled. "Then tell me," he said, "whether you feel you can actually execute the type of engraving you so skillfully designed in honor of the noted composer."

"The composer?"

"Ludwig van Beethoven."

"Ah, so that's it," I said. "You want a Beethoven motif. What is it? A romantic number or a comedy sketch? You want the figures to look like engravings? Well, I suppose it will cost some money, but——"

The little man held up the palm of a small, pudgy hand and clicked his teeth together. "No, no, no," he said, "there is a misunderstanding."

"Isn't it a revue? You mean it's a straight play——"

"I am not in the theater," the little man said with a brief, faint smile. "I am a—I am in the postage-stamp business."

I was confused. "Postage stamps? What does that have to do with me?"

The little man brushed my question aside with a flick of his fingers. "You *are* the Francis Lagrange who recently won second prize in the Swiss Beethoven competition?"

I nodded.

"Your design showed a complete knowledge of engraving techniques. You *are* an engraver?"

I nodded again. "Not by profession," I said. "My father was an engraver and he taught me. I've worked as an engraver, but primarily I'm a painter."

"Yes, of course." The little man paused, clicked his teeth again in another faint smile, and waved a hand about the room. "Evidently you are not making a success of it."

"No."

"And you have no aversion to money?"

"No serious aversion."

"Lots and lots of money?"

"The more money, the more frivolous the aversion."

The little man settled back comfortably in his chair, folded his hands in his lap, and gazed steadily at me. His eyes, I noticed, were very small, but black, sharp as needles. "Then what would you say," he murmured, "if I told you that there is a great deal of money to be made in postage stamps?"

"In selling them?"

"Of course," he said, "but one must have them to sell."

I began at last to understand what the little man was driving at. "Go on," I said.

"Last year, in Paris," the little man continued, "the sale of a large private collection of stamps was completed to a number of avid collectors, all world-famous philatelists. The collection, one of the greatest in the world, realized the total sum of more than 26,000,000 francs. You would agree that that is money?"

"I would agree."

"Of course it was a large collection, one of the largest in the world," the little man said. "However, the value depended not on the quantity but the quality of the merchandise."

"That's usually the case," I said.

The little man held up a hand and began ticking off items one by one. "There was a British Guiana 1856 one cent, a pair of Hawaiian Islands 1851 two cents, a Mauritius, a Baden, some United States postmaster issues dating back to 1846, a France 1849 fifteen cents. You have never seen any of these items?"

I shook my head.

"The British Guiana stamp alone is worth millions. It is supposed to be unique."

"And is it?"

"Not exactly," the little man said, smiling and clicking his teeth again. "Not exactly."

"There is a duplicate?"

"We have high hopes of providing buyers with duplicates of a few of these very rare stamps."

"I see."

"Very excellent duplicates, indistinguishable from the originals," the little man said. "Not too many of them, of course, and not sold indiscriminately. It would be a pity to flood the market. And the stamps must, of course, be of the highest quality. The workmanship must be not merely excellent, but perfect. You understand?"

"Go on."

"We will provide the materials, including the original stamps, and——"

"The originals? If you have the originals, why not sell them?"

The little man giggled. "We do not really own the stamps," he said. "They are usually supplied on loan from co-operative collectors."

"On loan?"

"There is enough money for everyone," the little man said, standing up. "I take it you are interested?"

I looked at him, trying to pierce behind the black, penetrating eyes, then I nodded slowly. "How much money?" I asked.

"It depends on the size of the job, Lagrange," the little man said. "For the engraver, the cut is usually twenty per cent of the sales price." He took a slip of paper from his pocket, scribbled a telephone number on it, and handed it to me. "Take your time," he said. "Don't rush. But when you've really decided, call this number."

"What's your name?"

"Joel," the little man said. "Whoever answers, always ask for Joel."

7 *Crime Never Pays Enough*

I DIDN'T telephone Joel until the following afternoon, not because I was wrestling with my soul or anything silly like that, but because Paulette and I staged such a celebration that I was unable to talk to anyone until then. As I mentioned earlier, I've always accepted life on its own terms. I regarded Joel's entrance into my studio as a stroke of incredible good fortune. He was to be the agent of my permanent release from the horrible bonds of poverty. No more cold, no more hunger, no more quarrels, no more naughty pictures, no more anything but warmth, love, and joy in my work. Goethe didn't know what he was talking about: when Dr. Faust sat down and sold his soul to the Devil, I think he got the better of the deal!

Every time I telephoned Joel, a different voice answered. Sometimes he was there, sometimes he wasn't, but he was always in touch with me within a few hours of my calls. I never made any attempt to talk to anyone else. I knew, of course, that Joel was working with a gang specializing in forgeries of different kinds, but I had no desire to learn any of the details of the operation or to meet any of my colleagues. The less I knew, the happier I was. I did my job and I asked no questions. My only contact with the gang was through Joel. It was he who told me what the job was, how it was to be done, who supplied me with the necessary materials, picked up and delivered the merchandise, paid me my twenty per cent commission and kept me posted on the progress of the gang's various operations. We played no games together. Our talk was always strictly confined to business—what, when, where, and how much. I never even bothered to find out what his last name was. I worked hard, Joel paid on time, and I began to live well.

At first I did nothing but stamps and I discovered that I was extremely talented. My Mauritiuses were particularly successful, but really not much better than my American postmaster issues. It was just that there seemed to be more of an immediate demand for the former. I made one superb Guiana stamp and I was anxious to try others, but Joel wouldn't let me. He had no feeling for the artistic aspect of it. "Don't be a fool, Lagrange," was his only comment, "how do you think we could sell two of them in one year? It would be like finding two Mona Lisas under the same bed."

I was really astonished by what people would pay for these tiny little bits of paper, crude in color and design, manufactured not even a hundred years before. What earthly good were they? What happiness could they bring? Could one eat or wear them or buy love with them? No. They could only be looked at, kept under glass, hardly even touched. I tried to imagine the people who would spend so much money to own a scrap of colored paper. I saw them all as thin, dried-up, elderly gnomes, fussy and ill-tempered, the sort of persons who live alone in large, luxurious houses, surrounded by valuable objects, sharing nothing, touching nothing, giving nothing away, using their money and their power to acquire more ob-

jects, more things no one could use. Joel's clients were the
Alberichs of the world, I decided, the hoarders and collectors,
the non-doers, the non-users. If they could be satisfied by sup-
plying them with the objects they desired, the scraps of paper
and the little bits of wood and the chunks of metal, why not
supply them? It made everyone happy and hurt no one. And
it was so easy to do.

After a few months, we began to branch out. As Joel put
it, the stamp market has its limitations; there aren't that many
valuable stamps and to concentrate on producing large numbers of the ones that are worthwhile can only lead to embarrassment and gloom. Imagine the pique of a collector who
thinks he has just acquired something unique and discovers
that it isn't! They set such store by numbers, these avid little
Alberichs! Values plummet and complaints are registered with
the authorities and happiness is dispelled, all for no reason.
One has only to be careful, to respect the psychology of the
collector, to understand his own particular numbers game and
allow him to play it. Otherwise he becomes annoyed and
troublesome.

I began to dabble in this and that, depending on what Joel
needed me for. I tried my hand at antiquities of various kinds
as well as a little *expertise*. Joel seemed to have a hand in several markets and he had connections with a couple of art galleries. I made old coins, broken statuettes, ancient furniture—
anything that paid. When the galleries needed an expert to
come in and convince a client of an object's authenticity, I
appeared, attired in the respectable mantle of my father's
name. Was this really an Etruscan coin? Yes, unquestionably,
I would say, turning the object over in my hands, often ad-
miring my own workmanship. Was this really a bit of frieze
from the Temple of Athena on the Acropolis? Undoubtedly,

I would say, remembering the hours I had spent on the delicate, graceful little figures. Was this chair actually the one Lucrezia Borgia sat in? Most certainly, I would answer, flourishing documents of authentication I had completed that very morning. Was this sketch truly by Cézanne? Of course, I would say, remembering the difficulties I had had with the anatomy of the seated man. It was all very amusing and profitable.

I was happiest with Gauguin, I think. Something in this great master's work had always appealed strongly to me, as if we shared a deep secret with each other. His feeling for the basic essence of light, for capturing flesh and fantasy in terms of light, using colors in a flat, almost brutal way, had always evoked in me a tremendous response. It was as if Gauguin, particularly in his tropical paintings, had anticipated the direction my own work was to take. His, of course, was by choice; mine was by compulsion. When Joel showed up in my studio one morning and asked me to try my hand at a couple of canvases by the master, I was delighted to oblige. Quite apart from the monetary profit I would derive, I was happy to think there would be more Gauguins in the world.

It seems odd to admit this now, but I can't remember exactly how many Gauguins I turned out. It was either four or five, but I can no longer be absolutely sure. Perhaps it's just as well that my memory is hazy on the subject, since my Gauguins were never discovered and are, as far as I know, still in various collections. Joel never told me to whom they were sold or for how much (I received a flat fee for each of these paintings), but it's probable that he didn't know himself. They were undoubtedly disposed of through one or more private dealers. The less one knows about the business end of these matters, the safer and happier one remains. The paintings were tropical in theme, not as large as the better-known Gauguins (no sense pushing one's luck and they had to be finished in a hurry), and appropriately titled. Beyond the fact that they all have naked women in them, I prefer to remain silent on the subject matter. After all, the paintings were sold, they exist, they're artistically authentic, and they bring some people pleasure. I hope they hang in a museum and not merely in some Alberich's private hoard.

We had a nasty moment or two with one of the paintings. A few days after I had completed it, Joel telephoned me. His voice was as cold and calm as ever, but there was a slight edge of panic to it. Was I aware of the horrible blunder I had committed?

"Blunder?" I asked. "What are you talking about?"

"You signed the painting."

"Well, of course I signed it."

Joel's calm deserted him. "With your own name, you idiot!" he screamed. "A beautiful Gauguin with your own insignificant, puny name in the corner! Idiot! If I hadn't looked at it. . . ."

Joel must have been very disappointed in me, because all I could do was shriek with helpless laughter. However, after hanging up on him, I had a mild case of the shakes. It would have been such a grotesque, absurd way to be caught. I decided to do no more Gauguins. I was too close to the man, too vulnerable. If I kept on, I would slip again, perhaps in a more dangerous way. I realized that I risked submerging my own identity in the master's work. It was a risk I was perfectly prepared to run (and I was running it every day) as a counterfeiter, but I was not prepared to run it in my own work. Because I had not given up the idea of my career as a painter. Forgery was my way of going to the office every morning; on my own time I painted. On my own time I continued to be Francis Lagrange, the undiscovered genius of Montmartre.

Strangely enough, the first casualty of my new life was Paulette. She turned out to have scruples. Instead of rejoicing in our new prosperity, she resented the source of it and allowed it to poison her feeling for me. At first she had been amused. She had sat in a corner of the studio and watched me at work, marveling at my skill, clucking and cooing over the final product of it. But she had thought the situation temporary. When she saw that I was perfectly prepared to continue forging and counterfeiting, when she saw me reveling in my first Gauguin, when she realized that the act of forgery itself gave me pleasure, she revolted. It turned out that she had a most conventional outlook on money. She was willing to spend it, she wasn't too fussy about where it came from, but she couldn't bear the idea that I *enjoyed* earning it, especially when this enjoyment was derived from doing something wrong.

I couldn't understand this attitude and I was entirely unsympathetic. I combated it by buying her things. She accepted everything I bought for her, even thanking me profusely, but she never ceased to reproach me. "To think that it would come to this!" she said one evening as I was finishing up an African wood carving. "That I should be living with a common criminal!"

"Not common," I said. "Very uncommon."

"My mother, my poor mother," she said. "If she had lived, what would she have done?"

"I imagine she would have wanted a cut of the profits," I answered coldly.

"And my father! What would he say!"

"Ask him. If you can find him. Have you checked all the hospitals and lunatic asylums?"

It was a magnificent brawl. I never would have believed that my slender, delicate Paulette could even lift the kitchen table, much less hit me with it. Or that her head was so hard it would split my wood carving at the very first blow. Of course the fight ended in the usual way, but for once our love-making failed to clear the air. We lay there side by side, nursing our wounds, disappointed at last in purely physical atonement. So I did a rash thing. I actually promised Paulette that I would stop working for Joel and try to become an honest man again, if one can say that working in the theater or painting naughty pictures is honest. But, alas, I had no intention of keeping my promise.

I compromised. Instead of working on my counterfeits at home, I rented another small studio and moved my equipment into it. I told Paulette that I had finished with Joel and I instructed him to contact me only at the new studio. As far as Paulette was concerned, I had turned respectable. Meanwhile, from my new lair, I continued to grind out my little frauds.

Paulette's attempt to reform me was her undoing, because, to make my double life truly authentic, I went back to the theater. The impresario who had given me my first set-designing job was mounting a new revue and he hired me again. On the second day of rehearsals, I showed up with a lot of sketches under my arm and walked down the aisle of the grubby little theater where a run-through was in progress. The impresario was sitting sullenly in the first row, watching a line of girls stumble through a horrible dance routine. I sensed that this was no time to show him anything and I sat down several rows behind him, waiting for a break or a more propitious moment to approach him. Idly, my eye ran down the line of girls and suddenly my attention was riveted. There, falling all over her feet and bumping into everyone, was the most beautiful girl I had ever seen.

She was also the worst dancer I had ever seen, with an absolute genius for creating chaos around her. She fell over her own feet and managed to step on everyone else's. Within seconds she had succeeded in clearing a wide area of the stage. Her ineptitude made no difference to me—I was hypnotized by her lovely figure, her soft blond curls, her wide, round, innocent blue eyes—but the impresario was beside himself. When he could stand no more of it, he bounded to his feet, screaming.

Most of what he shouted was incoherent, but a few words of the monologue did come through. The girl was fired. The impresario stormed out through the rear of the house, the other girls slowly, silently cleared the stage, and my poor lost beauty was left there all alone, dismayed, with large, round tears streaking her delicate cheeks. I rushed to the rescue.

Her name was Marilyn. She was twenty-two years old, she had been in Paris only a month, she wanted to become a musical-comedy star, and this had been her first job. Now what would she do? She was all alone, friendless, penniless. Where could she turn? The big, round tears dripped heartbreakingly into her coffee cup. I leaned over the table of the small café I had taken her to and I patted her lovely cheek. "Don't cry, my dear," I said, "I'll help you."

I went to a telephone and called up Joel. I explained the situation to him. He was unsympathetic. I insisted. "Joel," I said, "I know you can help. You know everyone, you have a finger in everything. Call up some of your friends."

"I haven't time, Lagrange. I'm a busy man."

"Make the time."

"Why should I?"

"Because I ask you to."

Joel snorted impatiently. "My dear Lagrange," he said, "do you think I'm going to go out and get every chippie you pick up a job?"

"Just this one."

"I'm sorry. It's impossible. I cannot allow your private life to interfere with business."

"Very well," I said, "then I won't allow your business to interfere with my private life." I started to hang up.

"Lagrange," Joel said, a note of alarm in his voice. "What do you mean?"

"We're all busy men," I said coldly. "I'm so busy I may not even have time to finish all the unfinished jobs I have in my studio."

There was a pause from the other end. "Call me back tonight," Joel said at last. "But tell me, Lagrange. . . ."

"Yes?"

"She's pretty?"

"Beautiful."

"Does she have any talent?"

"None whatever."

Joel groaned and hung up.

I went back to the table where Marilyn still sat, dabbing at her eyes. "Now you mustn't worry about anything," I said, squeezing her little hand. "It's all being arranged." She smiled through her tears and kissed me on the cheek. *Au revoir*, Paulette; *bon jour*, Marilyn.

Joel was kept very busy for weeks. He would find Marilyn jobs and she would dance her way out of them. No one, not even the resourceful Joel, could find a way to keep her from ruining a chorus line. Finally, a solution of sorts was found at the Folies-Bergère. Marilyn was hired to stand still and smile. This she managed to do supremely well.

My separation from Paulette was not easy. After all, we had been through some very bad times together and it seemed ironic that now, just when things were going better, it should all end so suddenly. Still, there was no help for it. I was hopelessly in love with the blond curls and the dimpled cheeks and the blue, blue eyes. I didn't try to fool Paulette. She deserved better than that from me. It is one thing to fool a woman on the source of money; it's quite another to fool her in matters of love. I could not have pretended to Paulette. I told her the truth.

It was a painful business. She heard me out in silence, not looking at me the whole time. When I had told her how it was, she stood up and went over to the window, staring down over the rooftops of Paris for a long, long moment. Finally, she turned back to me. "You really love her, Flag?" she asked me in a low, gentle voice.

I nodded helplessly.

"I see," she said. "Then there is nothing to be done, is there?"

That night she packed her things and moved out. After all the fights, all the tears and broken furniture and smashed crockery, I had expected a different kind of ending, a holocaust of some sort. It just shows how one can underrate a woman. Here was a matter too serious, too crucial for blows. Paulette understood that, even if I had not. At the door she kissed me one last time and walked out of my life. I sat in my room alone for a long time after she had gone, feeling absolutely wretched, fighting the impulse to go running out after her, to bring her back. Of course I could not do that. It could only have made things so much worse. Quiet endings are the most civilized and also the most terrible, I discovered.

From the moment Marilyn came into my life, I became dedicated to money. It was the only way I could keep her happy. Like Paulette, she had extremely expensive tastes, but, unlike Paulette, she didn't care at all where the money came from. We moved at once into a much more luxurious apartment in one of the most fashionable sections of the city, with a private studio where I continued to manufacture *objets d'art.* Marilyn paid no attention to my work. She only became excited if I was unable to afford what she most desired at the moment. She would accuse me of not loving her, of wanting to keep her in rags, of being ashamed of her, of bullying and mistreating her. She kept threatening to leave me. I didn't appreciate her. Tears, tantrums, implorations. Then, having obtained what she wanted, she would fall into my arms, squealing and cooing. She was like a very pretty, terribly spoiled child, and I couldn't resist her. With one hard practical eye I would look at her, evaluate her, compare her to Paulette, and find her wanting in every way; but with the other eye I was blind, hopelessly in love. We spent the money as fast as I earned it and, after a while, we spent it faster than I earned it. In a way, it was worse than being poor. With Paulette, I had had nothing; with Marilyn, I owed money.

The months passed and the debts mounted. I gave up my own painting and devoted my entire time to forgery. Unfortunately, there seemed to be a limit on what the market could absorb in every area. Joel was extremely cautious. He would only handle safe merchandise and only of a sort in immediate, unquestioned demand. He refused to push. Of course he was right. One Greek statue, one painting, one coin or stamp too many and we all risked catastrophe. But I was in no mood for caution. I was madly, hopelessly in love and I needed huge sums of money to cushion that love. I was not going to lose my

Marilyn, even if I had to make the money myself. Which is exactly what I began to do.

I came home from seeing Joel late one afternoon, still seething over his refusal to let me try just one more Guiana stamp. I was half a million francs in debt by this time and the Guiana stamp would have gone a long way toward getting me even. Marilyn was out shopping that afternoon, moving like a Mongol horde through every jewelry store in town, and who knew what my debts would be by nightfall. Filled with this gloomy thought, I was heading for my studio when a squat, bulky figure rose off my living-room sofa. "Lagrange," it said, in a strange, hoarse voice, "sit down! We must talk."

I looked at my uninvited visitor. He had an absolutely round head, hairless and badly scarred, no eyebrows, a flat nose, thick, brutal lips, and dark, heavy jowls. His eyes were very pale, like a snake's, and I had the odd notion that he could turn people to stone with them. I was afraid of him, I realized. "What do you want?"

"We must talk," the man repeated, gesturing brusquely at an armchair. "Sit down."

"Who are you?"

"You've heard of me, I think," the man said. "Delanoit."

Indeed I had heard of him. He was the most feared man of the Parisian underworld, with a fantastic reputation for ruthlessness. I had heard a story that he had once kicked a man to death in front of half a dozen witnesses and that no one had dared to raise a finger against him. He reportedly had a hand in every big deal. I sat down in a hurry.

"Let's not waste time," Delanoit said, jamming his hands into his pockets and fixing me with those pale, empty eyes. "What's your cut with Joel?"

I told him. He grunted, chewed on it for a minute or so,

then sat down directly opposite me. "Your stamps are good," he said. "One or two of them were not perfect, but you'll learn with time. With me, it's perfection or nothing, you understand?"

"You want me to make stamps for you?" I asked.

"No." He reached a hand into his pocket and threw a large wad of bills into my lap. "I want you to make those."

I thumbed through the bills. There were pound sterling notes of various denominations and American dollars in fifty and one hundred dollar bills. "Your cut will be the same as with Joel," Delanoit said, "but you'll work only for us."

"How will Joel feel about that?"

The pale eyes never wavered from mine. "How should he feel?" Delanoit said. "He'll go along."

"And if he doesn't?"

"He will. You let us worry about that." He stood up and pointed at the bills. "Take your time, Lagrange," he said. "We'll give you everything you need for the work. I want everything first-rate. With me it's perfection or nothing, you understand?"

"Yes."

"Joel is a nice boy but he's small-time. His vision is narrow and he's too afraid to become better than he is. You are a man who needs money." He stared around the room. "With me you'll have all the money you need. More than you need."

Knowing Marilyn's tastes, I was prepared to challenge that answer, but I saw no reason to upset Delanoit. We settled all the business details very quickly. Basically, the operation would be the same as with Joel. Delanoit and his gang would supply me with the necessary materials and make all the pickups and deliveries. After the counterfeit notes had been successfully changed, I would receive my twenty per cent cut.

I was given a number to call, a name to ask for, and other pertinent instructions. When Delanoit got up to leave, he tapped a blunt forefinger lightly against my chest. "Remember the arrangement, Lagrange," he said. "Don't get ideas."

"What kind of ideas?"

"Don't, for instance, make the mistake of believing that you can unload the merchandise without us."

"Why would I do that?"

Delanoit sighed. "Almost everyone gets that idea sooner or later," he said. "That's why I'm here today. We just lost our best manufacturer."

"What happened to him?"

Delanoit smiled. "He is crouching on the bottom of the Seine," he said, "in a tub of lard."

By the time Marilyn came home that evening, her new jewels clinking softly together, I was already in the studio, studying, under a strong overhead light, the intricacies of the British pound sterling and the American dollar.

8 Fra Bartolo

As Delanoit had predicted, Joel went along. In fact, I never saw or heard from him again. I didn't really miss him, because with my new connections I began to do much better. Even with the Gauguins and the stamps, working for Joel had not earned me what the merchandise deserved. Delanoit, on the other hand, was a big-time operator, with a large and very powerful organization at his back. He was able to handle just about anything and to cope with every aspect of an operation, from manufacture to distribution. Of course I was only a small wheel in that machine, but I soon became a very well-oiled one.

I hope I will not offend my Anglo-Saxon friends if I confess that I found the manufacture of both the pound sterling and the dollar to be mere child's play. After all, I was a highly trained and very expert engraver; the trick in counterfeiting is not the execution of the fake bill itself, but the obtaining of the proper materials—the right inks and, above all, the right paper. Delanoit's organization was able to supply everything I needed. After that, I merely had to be meticulously careful and observant in the execution of the bills. It turned out that I had a real gift for it. Within a couple of weeks, my first fake bills were in circulation. Within a month, I had become a millionaire.

This was very lucky for me, because Marilyn had become a veritable princess in her tastes. Nothing was too expensive. She always bought during the day whatever she had dreamed about the night before. I couldn't deny her anything. And, oddly enough, I couldn't really say any longer that I was in love with her. I had loved Maria, I had loved Paulette, I had loved one or two other women almost as deeply, but I felt something quite different for Marilyn. I was drugged by her; I needed to have her, not as a man needs a wife or a faithful mistress, but as an addict needs his dose of dope. I gave up everything for her, my whole life. I had not only stopped painting, I had even lost the desire to paint. She had become a habit, an obsession that would, perhaps, destroy me. I could be rational about her, I could even see very clearly what she had done to my life, but I could not give her up.

Though the rest of my life in crime was to be devoted exclusively to counterfeiting, I did carry out one last venture into art forgery—the most difficult and most interesting one of my entire career. Because the museum involved made every effort to hush the case up and, during the writing of this book, would not co-operate with me, refusing either to confirm or to deny the events, I have been advised not to use the actual names involved, not even that of the painter himself. That is why I have chosen to call him Fra Bartolommeo Lippi, a name that to the art connoisseur will provide enough clues for a proper identification of the old master in question. In any case, the story is authentic and can be verified by the discerning researcher. I present it now, disguised, but as it actually happened.

After I had been working for Delanoit for six or seven

months, he sent for me. He lived in a palatial house on the
Left Bank that had been converted into a fort. His gunmen
swarmed all over it and Delanoit himself could be reached only
by running a gantlet of hard-eyed bodyguards. I had never
seen him alone since that first night in my flat, when I hadn't
known who he was and he had had no need to fear me. Now
that we were in business together and owed each other things,
he was always attended by scrutable retainers, the sort of people who would break your fingers merely to while away a long
afternoon. On this particular occasion, he was, as usual, well-
attended, but he seemed glad enough to see me and quickly
waved the retainers away. Present in the room was a man I
hadn't met before, a prosperous-looking, chunky, bearded fellow in a dark, conservative business suit. Delanoit wasted no
time on preliminaries. "Lagrange," he said, "this is Van Botz.
He has a problem he wishes us to help him with. I think you're
the man."

Van Botz nodded to me and immediately outlined his problem. It was basically a simple one. He was an art dealer from
Amsterdam who numbered among his clients some of the
wealthiest private collectors in the world. These collectors
liked to deal with Van Botz because he was almost always able
to supply what was wanted. The collectors were not fussy
about the source if the object itself was genuine. Many of Van
Botz's objects were genuine; some of them had even been acquired legally. In fact, Van Botz assured me, he preferred to
deal in genuine objects. "Unfortunately," he said, spreading
his hands wide and smiling through the beard, "unfortunately,
this is not always possible."

"Don't waste our time," Delanoit growled. "Tell him what
you want."

Van Botz confessed that at the moment he found himself in

an embarrassing situation. One of his clients, an extremely
rich American from California, was most anxious to acquire
for his private collection a genuine work by a painter he admired enormously, a genius of the Italian *quattrocento*, Fra
Bartolommeo Lippi. Was I familiar with Lippi's work?

"Yes, very well," I said. "A very great master."

Delanoit grunted impatiently and filled the air with cigar
smoke. "Get to the point," he said.

The difficulty was that Van Botz found himself unable to
supply his client with the desired article. Lippi's works were
extremely rare and almost all of them were on view in public
galleries: the Uffizi in Florence, the National Gallery in London, the Louvre, the Berlin Museum, and so on. Because the
works were so rare and in such public display, it was impossible to buy them and almost equally impossible to steal them.
"And as for creating an original, the risk would be enormous,"
Van Botz said. "My American client is more of a snob than a
connoisseur, but he's a businessman and he would certainly
make every effort to check the authenticity of the painting. I
don't think we can fool him with a forgery. There hasn't been
an undiscovered Lippi on the market in many years. Entirely
too risky."

"If it's so risky," I said, "why are we bothering?"

"Because there's a hell of a lot of money in it, that's why,"
Delanoit said furiously.

Van Botz leaned forward in his chair. "My client is most
anxious to have his Lippi," he said. "Delanoit and I have come
up with a plan that we think will succeed. The success of it, of
course, depends on you to a very large extent. Do you think
you can make an exact copy—I should say a re-creation—of this
work?"

The dealer handed me several large, detailed photographs of

the work in question. It was a triptych of Lippi's, executed on copperplate, perfect in every detail and full of the Italian master's characteristically Gothic virtues. The center panel was a Madonna, already anticipating in its conception the later flowering of the Renaissance; in fact, it reminded me at once of Raphael's famous Dresden Madonna. The two smaller side panels depicted an Annunciation and a Nativity. I had never seen this triptych before, but I thought it a very lovely one and unquestionably authentic. I told Van Botz that I was reasonably certain I could do the job, but that I would need time and would have to have access to the original.

"That's quite easy," the dealer said. "The painting hangs in the Cathedral of R——. Or rather, in the small museum annexed to the cathedral. Of course the access is public, a rather serious handicap, but the museum is not heavily frequented and the painting itself hangs in one of the more secluded alcoves. How long do you think you will need?"

"I can't tell until I get there," I said.

"You have the time," Delanoit said. "We still have more than half your bills to unload. Go home and pack. You leave tonight."

Delanoit arranged everything with his customary efficiency. During my stay in R——, a large town in the North of France, I lived in one of the best hotels, within easy walking distance of the cathedral. A small attic room, cramped but with excellent light, was rented for me in a much less luxurious establishment across town, and it was there that I set up my atelier, taking the precaution to change the locks and to make sure that only I would have access to the room. Every day, at different hours, I would stroll into the museum of the Cathedral of R——, sketchbook in hand.

Van Botz had made a shrewd selection. The triptych was

easily accessible, isolated from the rest of the museum collection, and hung close enough so that I could capture every nuance of the artist's execution. However, it was slow work. I could not spend more than an hour or two a day in the museum without calling attention to myself. And the painting itself demanded the very best work from me. Day after day I copied it, piece by piece, detail by detail, running from the museum to my little workroom where, ever so slowly and meticulously, the Lippi triptych was being re-created.

There are a thousand tricks to the art of restoration and my father had taught me all of them. This was fortunate for me, because the restorer's profession is the only sure road to a successful career in forgery. In addition to the tricks and the skills (I am assuming the necessary talent on the part of the forger), one needs the proper materials. The paints used by Fra Bartolo and his contemporaries are not those of today. I had to compound them chemically out of basic substances that were supplied to me from Amsterdam, then the art-forging capital of the world and the seat of Van Botz's operations. But beyond mere talent, the tricks, the possession of knowledge, and the ability to obtain the proper materials, the really great forger must have something else, something no one can teach him, something that has little or nothing to do with technique. He must have the ability to project himself into another man's skin, to destroy his own personality, and to submerge himself in another's identity. His own creative talents are of no significance. One thinks immediately of Van Meegeren, a mediocre painter in his own behalf but a man capable of turning out original masterpieces by Vermeer. The forger's genius, brought to its highest pitch of perfection, is a slightly sinister, almost mystical thing, as if the soul of the original artist were seeking to return to life through it. I possessed this genius. There were moments in that atelier when, submerged in the re-creation of Fra Bartolo's masterpiece, I actually forgot who I was. If anyone had opened the door and burst in on me, I might conceivably have addressed him in Italian!

It took me about two months to finish the job. Van Botz then came down to have a look at it, bringing with him an ancient German expert of undoubted skill and dubious reputation. The ancient German examined the painting very carefully and pointed out a couple of minor flaws in two or three of the ornamental details, which I immediately went to work on. After I had corrected them, a simple task, the German announced his approval.

All that now had to be done to the painting was to age it, a process that was accomplished in a matter of minutes under my very eyes. The ancient German produced a kind of air gun, aimed it at the triptych, and fired. Soon all three panels were beautifully coated by a special varnish that imparted to the painting the exactly correct look of age and wear. We stood in front of it, in silent admiration. Then the ancient German put away his gun and I poured us some wine to celebrate the occasion.

"A brilliant job, Lagrange," Van Botz said. "Do you know what the painting is worth?"

"It's listed in one of the catalogues at 750,000 francs," I said. "I suspect that on the open market it will be worth more."

"Considerably more," Van Botz said contentedly. "My client is ready to pay up to 5,000,000 for it."

"Are you taking it with you tonight?"

Van Botz smiled. "I told you in Paris, Lagrange, that we could not risk a forgery, especially for such a large sum and for this type of merchandise. My client will have the piece scrupulously examined. As you know, there are ways now of telling. . . ."

"I don't understand," I said. "Then what——"

"My dear Lagrange," Van Botz said, patting me on the shoulder, "you should be proud. You are about to be hung in the museum of the Cathedral of R——."

I don't think I shall ever cease to marvel at my own innocence in those days. It had never even occurred to me that Van Botz and Delanoit intended all along to steal the original Lippi. Perhaps, if I had known, I wouldn't have gone through with the job. Out of cowardice, I admit, not because of any misplaced scruples. I had been involved in the world of crime for only about three years, but my scruples had not withstood the test of a single day.

Needless to say, I did not carry out the exchange of art works myself; in fact, I prudently returned to Paris that very evening. Sometime during the next couple of days, two of Delanoit's staff of specialists, experts in the field of illegal entry, came from Paris, broke into the museum, removed Fra Bartolo's triptych from the wall, and substituted Lagrange's.

Day after day I scanned the newspapers, expecting at any moment to read that the daring crime had been discovered. I couldn't believe that my forgery, good as it was, could be exposed to the public gaze and not eventually be detected. But nothing happened. A week went by, then another. Finally, an emissary arrived from Delanoit with my share of the sales proceeds: 800,000 francs! The original Lippi, I was told, had been smuggled out through Holland and sold to the millionaire from California, no questions asked, for about 4,000,000 francs. A nice job of work, I had to admit.

Well, I said to myself, that's that. I resumed my luxurious Parisian life with Marilyn and tried to turn my attention to the future. However, a strange thing began to happen to me; I couldn't seem to put the Lippi Madonna out of my mind. I even started to dream about her. She became an obsession, filling my days and nights with her image. Nothing like it had ever happened to me before and, with every ounce of strength, I resisted this siren. I could not, I would not yield to the impulse that soon became an almost intolerable craving. Marilyn complained bitterly that my nights were filled with monomaniacal discussions, tossings, and turnings, loud but rational appeals to my own powers of common sense. I *could* not, I *would* not go back! It was madness, idiotic, foolish! Criminals did not return to the scenes of their crimes, everyone knew that! I took sleeping potions, I figuratively bound myself to the bed. Nothing worked. The calm, inscrutable face of my Madonna lured me irresistibly back, back, back. When I could stand it no longer, I leaped out of bed early one morning, hastily packed a bag, and rushed off to R——.

Face to face with my Madonna again, hanging there in her accustomed niche in the museum of the Cathedral of R——, I experienced an extraordinary feeling of peace, of deep satisfaction. I was not, I hasten to add, the beneficiary of a religious miracle; my forged Madonna was making no attempt to reform me. I suffered no remorse and I had no urge to rush off and denounce myself to the police. The peace, the satisfaction I felt was due to something quite different. Partly, of course, it was simple pride in the accomplishment of a difficult job; partly it was sheer delight in the success of a huge joke; and partly, too, it was pure vanity. But to a large extent it sprang from a belief that my own talent had been vindicated at last. During those months of waste with Marilyn, I had lost confidence in myself as an artist. I had become a forger, first and foremost—a man exercising a skill for a purely monetary reward. To my Lippi, on the other hand, I had brought not only skill but dedication and love. I was as proud of that Madonna as if I had conceived her myself.

I found that I was unable to leave R——. Once again, every day, at different hours, I would stroll into the museum and halt in front of the triptych to bask in my own glory. The experience was not without its comic moments. Groups of tourists would stroll past or pause beside me to gaze at the picture. Marvelous, *wunderbar*, *formidable*, they would exclaim. These painters of the Middle Ages are inimitable. What modern artist could turn out such a masterpice?

One day I found myself standing next to a stout, middle-aged German with a sweaty, beet-red face and cropped iron-gray hair. He was the typical German tourist, dressed in heavy walking shoes, khaki shirt and shorts, burdened with cameras and afire with aggressive, humorless enthusiasm. He banged me with his elbow. "Look, look," he said in guttural French, "what magnificent art work! What feeling for detail!" He aimed a camera at the triptych as if it were a cannon and squeezed the trigger. "What a glorious masterpiece! No one paints that way today, my friend. That is because no one *can* paint like that today. I am right, no?"

"No," I said quietly. "I paint like that."

The German lowered his camera and looked at me. "You are joking?"

"No, I'm not joking."

"You mean you *try* to paint like that."

"And I succeed."

The German's face began to bake and steam. "You are French," he said. "The French cannot paint like the Italians, the Dutch, and the Germans. The French are all Impression-

We had no idea what was in store for us as we marched for the first time into the camp of St. Laurent.

ists and Impressionism is the decay of true art. You cannot paint a Lippi."

"Yes, I can. I have." I waved carelessly at the painting. "I painted that one."

The German stared at me out of bulging, maddened eyes. "You French," he said angrily, "such conceit! One day we Germans will teach you a lesson you will not forget. The German nation will know how to deal with this decadent people. We will. . . ."

Well, what was I to do? I had spoken the truth and I had not been believed. I could have remained there the rest of my life, telling tourists that I had painted that Madonna, not Fra Bartolo, and no one would ever have believed me. Eventually, perhaps, I might have been taken away to rot in some lunatic asylum, still vainly protesting the true authorship of my Madonna. What makes crime possible, and especially the crime of forgery, is that people will believe only what they wish to believe; they will accept almost anything on blind faith alone. Tell a man that the rusty old nail you hold in your hand is actually one of the nails used to crucify Jesus and the chances are nine out of ten that he will believe you. I knew then that, as far as the forgery itself was concerned, I had absolutely nothing to worry about.

However, when I got back to the hotel that afternoon, one of Delanoit's gunmen was waiting for me in the lobby. I had been in R—— for about ten days, Delanoit had become alarmed, and the gunman had been told to make sure that I left town before anyone became suspicious. I knew now that there was little danger on that score, but I had no desire to join my predecessor on the bottom of the Seine. I packed my bag and allowed the gunman to drive me out of R—— in one of Delanoit's automobiles. On the way, I did persuade him to stop

Life inside the camp was not much better
and not much worse than life in the army.

briefly by the museum and I paid a hurried final call on my
Madonna.

"Well, Fra Bartolo," I said, smiling up at the painting for the
last time, "you can't say I didn't do you justice."

Fortunately for me, Fra Bartolo did not answer.

But, alas, there is no such thing as the perfect crime. No
matter how carefully one plans and executes a job, there is
never any protection against the unforeseen coincidence. One
builds a complicated, delicate mechanism, makes certain that
every part of it functions perfectly, takes the trouble to grease
and oil every cog within it, and the inevitable, accidental grain
of sand, wafted into the works by some passing, stray gust of
wind, destroys it as surely, as effectively as if a stick of dyna-
mite had been planted under it. My grain of sand, my unforeseen coincidence was the American stock-market crash of 1929.

The gentleman from California who had paid such a generous price for his Lippi was, like so many of his fellow capital-
ists, wiped out overnight. He found himself obliged to sell his
large and valuable collection of masterpieces and the sale was
entrusted to a large British auction house. Thus it was that,
some eighteen months later, when the director of the museum
of the Cathedral of R—— happened to be glancing idly one
day through the latest English auction-house catalogues, he
made the startling discovery that his prized triptych was being
offered for sale in London.

The director was a man of action. Without bothering to
check the authenticity of his own painting, he hurried off to
London to denounce the American's triptych as a forgery. To
his amazement, he was confronted by a battery of formidable
experts, all of whom assured him that the American's picture
was unquestionably authentic. Stunned, the director rushed
back to R——, summoned experts of his own, removed my

Madonna from its place of honor on the museum wall, and submitted it to a meticulous examination. The verdict was soon
in and the director of the museum of the Cathedral of R——
took the only course left open to him: he summoned the police.

The police in those days were not very brilliant in such
matters, but the case was so unusual that they took extraordinary precautions. A meticulous investigation was instituted,
involving detectives of four nations. (The Dutch, the English,
and the Germans had long been aware of the existence of an
international art-forging and smuggling ring and they collaborated with the French on this case.) And, as always, it was a
minor oversight, the coincidental grain of sand, that undid me.

In making a routine check of all hotels and lodginghouses
over the past few years, a bored detective found himself ques-
tioning one day the owner of the fleabag establishment where
I had rented my tiny attic room. The list of guests had yielded
nothing of interest. Could *Monsieur le propriétaire* remember
anything on his own, anything unusual about any one of his
guests during this period? No, *Monsieur* could not. The detective thanked *Monsieur* and prepared to leave. One moment,
said *Monsieur,* it is probably nothing, but perhaps the detective would be happy to see something very lovely. *Monsieur
le propriétaire* rummaged through his papers and produced
his prize. It was a small scrap of paper with a sketch of a delicate female hand on it and, underneath the hand, there was
a scribbled notation: "Be careful of the second finger and the
contrast with the robe at this spot." Was it not lovely, *Monsieur le propriétaire* demanded? Of course it could have no
bearing on a police investigation, but he wanted the inspector
to know that he was a sensitive man, a person who appreciated
the finer things, and so he had conserved this little drawing
executed by one of his guests at the hotel. And where had

Monsieur found the drawing? Why, beside the stove, partly
burned. The gentleman who had occupied the attic room had
always had a fire every night, even in the warmest weather.
Indeed, the inspector said, how interesting. And what was the
name of this gentleman? Villard, *Monsieur le propriétaire*
said, Georges Villard, a very nice gentleman, so quiet and polite, such a pleasant guest and no trouble at all because he
never slept in his room at night, painters keep such odd hours,
of course the inspector understood, being a man of the world,
and he, *Monsieur le propriétaire*, did not mind in the least,
even when *Monsieur* changed the lock on the door and insisted
on having his own key, yes, well, these artists. . . .

The rest was easy. The police checked the handwriting of
the note against the signatures in other hotel registers and
matched it with my name. A warrant was immediately issued
for my arrest, but by that time it was too late. I was already in
jail, awaiting trial for a much more serious crime.

I am happy to say that the Cathedral of R—— was eventually able to reclaim its masterpiece, but not without difficulty.
Despite the official protests of the French Government, acting
on behalf of the director of the museum, the Lippi triptych was
sold to a Brazilian collector who donated it to *his* museum.
Finally, an exchange of art works was arranged. The French
Government allowed the Brazilians to purchase several lesser
works of the same period and the Lippi Madonna was rein-
stalled in her usual place, where, for all I know, she still hangs.

The Lippi triptych was my biggest and last art forgery. It
earned me a great deal of money, but, more important, it
brought me an immense amount of personal satisfaction. After
it, there was never another period in my life when I lost the
faith that I was capable of painting well. Not even Marilyn
could now keep me from my work, I thought.

9 Article 139

A few months after my return from R——, I made the break with Delanoit. I had no desire to die, but Marilyn's extravagance left me no choice. I either had to go into business for myself or sink permanently into a vast sea of debts. The only alternative was to leave Marilyn, which, I am ashamed to say, I never even contemplated. I had an interesting interview with Delanoit, whom I confronted in his armed palace with the news of my defection.

"No one walks out on this operation, Lagrange," he said, transfixing me with those pale eyes.

"I'm sorry," I said. "You've always played square with me, Delanoit, and I appreciate it, but I've got to do this. I have no choice."

There was a brief silence while Delanoit studied my face. "You will have a short life, Lagrange," he said.

I shrugged and made a ghastly effort to smile, affecting an indifference I did not feel. "Perhaps, but it can't be helped. Killing me, Delanoit, will solve nothing."

Delanoit grunted noncommittally.

"If I stay with you," I continued, "I'll be arrested for non-payment of debts. Is there anything more ridiculous than that? My only chance is to make some money on my own."

"You can't do that, Lagrange," he said. "How will you change the money? You don't have any organization. I do."

"I'm not going to make foreign money any more, Delanoit."

The pale eyes focused on me with renewed interest. "No?"

"I'm going to make francs."

Delanoit stood up. "Don't be a damn fool, Lagrange," he said angrily. "That's life imprisonment if they catch you."

"If."

"Without an organization in back of you, they'll catch you."

"You want to handle my francs? If you do, I want fifty per cent, not twenty."

Delanoit walked away from me, then turned back and jabbed at me with one of those huge, blunt fingers of his. "No," he said firmly. "No, I'm not going to handle your francs, Lagrange. The French are too serious about money. Their own money, not other people's. You go on making your dollars and pounds, Lagrange, and try to market them without me and I'll fix you for good. As I told you, no one walks out on this operation, no one. But if you're going to be a goddamn fool and make francs and get yourself put away for life, I'll do nothing, absolutely nothing to stop you. And you know why not?"

"No."

"Because they're sure to catch you, that's why, and when they do catch you, they'll put you away for keeps. We French do not play games with money. No one has ever made French bank notes for very long, Lagrange. Somehow they always get caught. Money is too much in the blood here."

"I'm going to try, Delanoit."

He sat down again and surveyed me more calmly. "All right, you fool, go ahead," he said, jabbing at me again. "But let me tell you something. When they do catch you, keep quiet. There isn't a prison in France I can't get to you in. You understand me?"

"I think so."

"Now beat it," he said, waving me out.

At the door, he stopped me again. "Lagrange!" I turned back. "Listen," he said, "I had a woman like yours once. You know what I did? I changed her face for her. You want me to do it for you? I can do it for you if you say so, Lagrange."

"If you even touch her, Delanoit," I said, "I'll find a way to kill you." Amazingly enough, I meant it, too. His threat had taken all the native cowardice out of me.

Delanoit looked at me and laughed. "Go on," he said, shooing me away. "Get out of here, you poor, sad fool. It makes me cry just to look at you."

If I had been able to face the truth in those days, I would have realized at once that Delanoit was right. The French Government doesn't really mind counterfeit foreign money, but it has no sense of humor at all about its own legal tender. If my operation with Delanoit had been discovered, I'm sure I would have been treated far more leniently than I was when I was put on trial for making French bank notes. The state can't bear competition, especially since it is itself the largest forger of counterfeit notes. Every bill issued by the government is supposed to be redeemable in gold, but everyone knows that this is a pure fiction. And since it is a pure fiction, the government's money is as worthless, in an ultimately realistic way, as the clumsiest private forgery. I'm not attempting to justify my own criminal position, but I do wish to point out that there is something particularly vindictive in the government's treatment of native counterfeiting, as if the state were admitting its own guilt in the matter.

However, such considerations did not trouble me at the

time. Once free of Delanoit, I set about organizing my own independent operation. A number of serious problems had to be solved, not the least of which was the manufacture of the money itself. We French have many faults, but no one will deny that we are an intelligent and complicated race, subtle in our perceptions and devious in our intellectual processes. These qualities are reflected, appropriately enough, in our money, which is full of pictorial nuances, tiny, maddening ornamental details, infinite subtleties of shading and color. It was weeks before I was able to turn out anything approximating a genuine bank note, several months before I was able to risk putting any of my money into circulation. Nevertheless, I persevered and eventually I was turning out perfect French bills in several sizable denominations. Within two or three months of my entrance into competition with the Bank of France, I had paid off all my debts.

The risk I ran was considerable and I was very much aware of it right from the start. For practical reasons, I made bills only in the larger denominations and these could be changed only in banks and other official or semi-official places of business, where money is submitted to a constant and careful scrutiny. But I had no choice, really. Making money in smaller denominations was out of the question, since Marilyn and I had by this time become accustomed to living like Oriental potentates. Needless to say, she spent my money as fast as I made it, which was considerably faster than prudence demanded. And to remind me of the risk I was running, every day I was compelled to print and re-read the ominous words that appear in a small box on every French bank note of whatever denomination: ARTICLE 139 OF THE PENAL CODE PUNISHES WITH FORCED LABOR THOSE WHO COUNTERFEIT OR FALSIFY BANK NOTES AUTHORIZED BY THE LAW.

However, as time passed and I continued to operate successfully, I acquired confidence and began to feel more secure. I had organized everything with extreme care, making certain that every aspect of my operation functioned smoothly, and I was meticulous about the appearance of the money itself. No bill was ever put into circulation that wasn't microscopically perfect in every detail. And I made certain that not too much money was ever changed at any one time in any one place. I had, I thought, prepared for every eventuality. I knew that it could not go on forever, but I had already formulated a plan. I would, after a year or so, make one final, tremendous coup, changing millions of francs in various different places, and then Marilyn and I would escape to South America. Quixotic as the idea now seems to me, I believed in it absolutely, though I wasn't ever quite sure how I would manage to persuade Marilyn to abandon her beloved Paris. In any case, my life seemed to have stabilized itself, we were living fantastically well, and I was certain that Marilyn adored me. I was blissfully unaware, of course, of stock-market developments abroad. Or of the lovely tricks fate can play on all of us, despite our most careful plans.

I was on my way home late one afternoon, strolling contentedly along the Champs-Elysées, when I was accosted by a haggard young prostitute with the usual invitation. Without even so much as glancing at her, I brushed her aside and walked on. I hadn't gone more than a few steps when something made me turn around. The girl had stopped in the middle of the path and also turned back. We stared at each other. It was my old flame, Paulette.

I went up to her at once and embraced her. She was obviously glad to see me, but terribly embarrassed. She was very thin, she looked ill and very much older, pathetic, and out

of place in the tawdry trappings of her new profession. "My
God, Paulette!" I said. "What's happened to you? I didn't even
recognize you!"

She smiled. "And I didn't recognize you, Flag. You've
changed as much as I have in these two years, but with you
it's obviously been for the better."

I took her to a bar and she brought me up to date on her life.
Since leaving me, it had been nothing but a series of disasters.
There had been two other men, both of whom had walked out
on her; she had lost her job and been unable to find another;
then she had fallen in with a third man, a pimp, who had
maneuvered her into prostitution. She had tried to escape from
it several times, but she had never been able to save the money
to do it. Then she had become ill and what she did make had
to go into medical care. "And here I am," she said, with a bitter
smile. "Not like the old days, eh, Flag? You wouldn't like me
now, I suppose." She looked at me wonderingly. "And with
you it goes well, eh?"

I nodded and told her about Marilyn and some of the things
I had been doing. I didn't have to go into any details with
Paulette; she could easily have guessed what I was up to. I
was suddenly embarrassed for myself as well as for her. "Listen," I said, taking her hand across the table, "you're going to
come home with me, right now."

Paulette shook her head. "Oh, no. I couldn't do that."

"Why not?"

"You don't owe me anything, Flag," she said. "I got myself
into this mess. You don't have to do anything."

"Come on," I said. "I'm not going to let you refuse. We have
a big house, there's plenty of room and money and you can
stay until you get yourself settled, as long as you like."

"But what about Marilyn, Flag? Won't she mind?"

"She'll understand," I said. "I'll explain it to her."

To my surprise, Marilyn did give every evidence of under-standing. She immediately welcomed Paulette into the house-hold, showed her every consideration, and treated her with sympathy and respect. I was proud of her. On her part, Pau-lette did everything she could to make herself useful to us, be-having toward both of us like a loving and devoted sister. Within a week, she and Marilyn were chattering away like a couple of very old, giggling school chums. In my masculine obtuseness I was certain that everything was working out just splendidly.

During the ensuing weeks, Paulette became almost indis-pensable to me, acting as a combination secretary and house-keeper. She performed all the onerous tasks of a devoted and loving wife that Marilyn had always ignored. There was no question ever of my resuming my old relationship with her and, in fact, I'm certain that the idea never occurred at any time to either of us, but I was delighted to have her around and I spoke glowingly of her to Marilyn. I was suddenly in the enviable position of being able to enjoy all the practical benefits of mar-riage and the delights of irresponsible love with none of the tedious drawbacks of either. I was just enough of a fool to be-lieve that it could go on like that forever.

Paulette came to see me in private one morning. She was pale and upset. "I'm leaving here, Flag," she said.

I was glancing through the newspaper and I didn't pay much attention to her. "Leaving? Nonsense! What for?"

"Because Marilyn is jealous of us."

I looked up from the paper and laughed at her. "Don't be ridiculous, Paulette. Why should she be jealous?"

"I don't know why, but she is."

"Did she say anything to you?"

"Yes. She came to my room last night and made a scene."

"And what did you do?"

She shrugged. "What could I do, Flag? She wouldn't listen to me. I told her I'd go."

I was angry by this time. "Well, you're not going to leave and that's that," I said. "I'll talk to Marilyn. I've never heard anything so ridiculous."

Marilyn said nothing to me when I berated her for her behavior to Paulette. I told her in no uncertain terms that Paulette would stay and that I wanted no repetition of the incident in future. She looked at me silently in a strange, oddly detached way, then flounced indignantly from the room. I dismissed the whole affair from my mind.

I can't deny that I should have realized what was bound to happen, but I resolutely refused to acknowledge every warning sign. The entire atmosphere of the house began to change. Paulette and Marilyn became frigidly polite to each other. I leaned more and more on Paulette and became increasingly impatient with Marilyn's childish behavior and extravagance. I was still horribly in love with her, but her vices, thrown into stark relief against Paulette's virtues, became intolerable to me. I made the very serious mistake of starting to compare her to Paulette, of holding Paulette up as an example to her. We had some lovely scenes.

Finally, the day came when Marilyn entered my studio unexpectedly and found me kissing Paulette. It was a perfectly innocent business. I don't even remember what the exact occasion was. I had given Paulette something or she had given me something and the kiss had been a completely spontaneous gesture of gratitude and affection. Marilyn took it all in, turned around, slammed the door, and rushed out of the house.

"You'd better go after her, Flag," Paulette said.

I laughed. "Don't worry about her," I said. "She'll go out and buy herself something to console her and by tonight it will all be forgotten."

At seven o'clock that evening Marilyn had still not come home. I had just begun to fret about her when the front doorbell rang. Standing on my stoop was a man in civilian clothes with two *gendarmes* at his back. "*Monsieur* Francis Lagrange?"

"Yes."

"You are under arrest. Article 139 of the Penal Code, *Monsieur.*"

They escorted me back through the house and went directly into my studio. They knew exactly what to do. They ripped out several rows of books and found most of the plates I had used to make my fake bank notes. A careful search of the rest of the house turned up two bundles of brand new bills I had been planning to put into circulation over the coming week. Paulette, I am glad to say, had gone out. As far as I know, she was never arrested and I never saw her again. By midnight I was behind prison bars.

10 *The End of a Road*

*T*HE lawyer assigned to my defense by the state was insistent on one point. It was absolutely necessary, he said, that I accuse Marilyn of complicity in my life of crime. "That way," he explained, "I'll be able to claim that you were blinded by your love for this woman and enslaved by her desires. It's the only defense I can make, Lagrange."

I knew that he was right, but I could not denounce Marilyn. During the six months I spent in jail awaiting trial I made an odd sort of peace with myself. I became completely resigned to my fate, even relieved. It was as if I realized at once that I had arrived at the inevitable end of a short and dangerous road. And long before I was actually brought to trial I had also been indicted for the Fra Bartolo affair. What was now to be gained by ruining Marilyn's life as well as my own? She would suffer the rest of her days for what she had done to me; there was no need to punish her for my crimes as well. The lawyer, poor man, threw up his hands in despair and prepared to throw us upon the mercy of the court.

While I was still in Paris and under the jurisdiction of the Tribunal of Versailles, poor Marilyn came to see me. She was in a pitiable condition, drunk, awash with remorse and guilt.

What could I say to her? I told her to take care of herself, to remember me with kindness, to look up Paulette and make sure that she was all right. Marilyn promised and promised and shed an ocean of tears at my feet. I kissed her on the cheek and watched her being led away. That was the strangest part of it all; I felt nothing any more for her but pity.

During the first weeks of my imprisonment the police came often to question me. They evidently knew nothing of my earlier operations with Joel and Delanoit, but they were unable to understand how it had been possible for me to work alone. How, for instance, had I been able to get the right paper? The chemical composition of the paper used to make French money is, as it is in other countries, a closely guarded secret and the paper itself is not, for obvious reasons, available on the local market. The accepted method of securing adequate supplies of paper for counterfeiting purposes is to highjack a government truck on its way to or from the mint, but there were no records of any such thefts during the past two years. The police could understand that any skillful engraver could make a reasonably good plate, but how had I been able to acquire exactly the right paper?

At first I wouldn't tell them, because I could see no advantage to me in doing so. However, they were naturally extremely anxious to pin down my source of supply and eventually they promised to intervene on my behalf with the judiciary authorities if I would co-operate. I decided to do so.

I don't know what secret they had expected me to reveal. Perhaps they had envisioned a vast underground network operating in conjunction with a corrupt treasury official or some such nonsense. When I did tell them the truth, they were flabbergasted by the direct simplicity of my method.

As a front for my entire operation, I had opened a very small

printing and engraving establishment on an obscure side street
of the city. I had printed up elaborate official stationery: "Francis Lagrange, Luxury Printing and Engraving, Personal Stationery Made to Order Only." Then I had begun to place
orders for different kinds of very expensive paper with a
number of well-established but small foreign manufacturers
in countries such as Czechoslovakia, Rumania, and Finland.
These orders were sizable and sometimes complicated to fill.

I would send along samples of the paper I needed, perhaps
thirty or forty different kinds. These samples were small, thin
strips, all of the same size and carefully mounted on a piece
of cardboard with the required amount of each type of paper
marked underneath each sample. Need I point out that one
sample in each batch had been clipped from the margin of a
brand new genuine bank note?

I had envisioned quite accurately what would happen. The
manufacturer would receive the order and match up the samples with the various kinds of readily available paper he had
in stock. He would doubtless find two or three samples not in
stock, but, being a small manufacturer and anxious to please
a client, he would summon his chemists and instruct them to
analyze the new samples and give him estimates of production
cost. These estimates would be forwarded to me, I would write
back confirming the entire order, and the manufacturer would
go ahead and make the paper. Eventually, large boxes of different kinds of paper would begin to arrive at the small store on
the obscure side street, and among the boxes would be the only
kind of paper that really interested me at all. By the time I
was arrested, I was receiving paper from all over the world
and there were at least three factories in Europe making sizable amounts of the special secret paper used by the Bank of
France.

At first the police wouldn't believe me, so I took them to my little shop where they found cartons of the paper as well as several tons of other types of paper. Did I mind, the officers wanted to know, what became of all this other useless paper? I said no, why should I mind? The officers telephoned for a truck and began to snatch up boxes and mark them with their own names. I'm sure that there are still people all over France, mostly the relatives of policemen, who are writing each other letters on my beautiful stationery.

I had already been in jail about four months when the Lippi affair broke. I was immediately subjected to further exhaustive interrogation, since the police knew very well that in this case I could not possibly have operated alone, but I kept my inner eye firmly fixed on the benevolent countenance of dear old Delanoit. I remembered my predecessor, probably still in his tub of lard at the bottom of the Seine, and I did not talk. When Delanoit had said that he could get to me in any prison in France, I was prepared to take him absolutely at his word. I insisted to the police that I had handled the Fra Bartolo transaction entirely on my own and nothing would shake me from this assertion.

Except for the tiresome hours of interrogation, I found that I really didn't mind prison life at all. Yes, it was dirty and uncomfortable, and the food was bad, but there were no responsibilities. The conduct of my life had been taken out of my hands entirely and, with my happy gift for making the appropriate psychological adjustment, I relaxed and enjoyed it as much as I could.

I became quite friendly with a dried-up little pickpocket named Leblanc, who shared my cell for several weeks. He was a four-time loser and expected to be sent permanently to Guiana, probably to the camp at St. Jean, where most of the *relégués* were quartered. He didn't mind at all, having grown too old and clumsy to exercise his nimble profession with any skill, and he was even looking forward to the tropical climate. "Ah, Lagrange," he said to me, "it's a sad thing for a pickpocket to have rheumatism. Look at these fingers, my friend, I can't even wiggle them properly. It'll take a year of sun to burn the clammy streets of this city out of me. I'm glad to go."

It was Leblanc who told me the story of Fernand, the clever counterfeiter who actually outwitted the law. "He was a great counterfeiter, my friend," Leblanc said. "He made perfect bills, just as good as yours in every way. I knew him well and I saw many of them. But he would only make them in the very small denominations. Never anything large."

"He must have had to make a lot of them," I said.

Leblanc smiled and shook his head. "Not many, my friend, not many. He was a man of simple tastes, you know. Happily married. No mistresses. Well, as I say, he made these perfect bills. That is, they were perfect in all except one small detail."

"What was that?"

"When it came time to fill in the little box that reproduces the Article 139, you know what Fernand did? He left that little box blank, absolutely blank."

"Why, he must have been caught right away," I said, astonished.

"Oh, not right away, my friend," Leblanc continued, "not right away. You see, old Fernand, he understood human psychology. He knew that hardly anyone ever looks carefully at a small bill, only at the large ones. Fernand knew that it would be months before anyone noticed that the little box on each of his bills was empty."

I still didn't understand. "But if his money was so good," I said, "why didn't he include the Article?"

"Because Fernand knew that one day he would be caught anyway," Leblanc said. "No matter how perfect the money is, my friend, one is always caught in the end, eh? Look at you. And when Fernand was caught, do you know what happened?"

"No."

"He claimed that, because he had never included the Article 139 in any of his bills, he was not guilty of having made counterfeit money," Leblanc said, hardly able to contain his mirth. "Old Fernand told the court that he had simply printed his own original money and that he could not be held responsible if people chose to accept his own currency instead of the state's." Leblanc rocked from side to side with laughter.

"He didn't get away with it?"

"He got six months and a suspended sentence, Flag. And what about you, eh? What are you going to get with that perfect money of yours?"

I had occasion to reflect on old Fernand's story. In January 1931 I was transferred to the jurisdiction of the Tribunal of R—— and finally brought to trial. In the face of the overwhelming evidence against me and my own admission of guilt, there was nothing my lawyer could do. For my activities as a counterfeiter I was sentenced to life imprisonment, and for the Lippi affair to ten years, the sentences to be served concurrently (a thoughtful touch on the part of the court!) in the penal colonies of French Guiana. This sentence was later reduced to twenty years because of my military service during the war and, later still, to fifteen years by an on-the-spot dispensation of the Special Tribunal in Cayenne. As Delanoit had told me, the French have no sense of humor about money.

11 *Hello, St. Laurent, Good-by*

I SHOULD have been dismayed by the severity of the sentence. Standing there, face to face with the stern expressions of my judges, hearing the terms of that fateful pronunciation read aloud, I should have experienced a quite natural feeling of despair. However, the truth is that I felt nothing but relief, as if the sentence itself marked not the end of my life but its beginning. I listened to the words spoken in the R—— courtroom with the utmost detachment and stoicism. I must confess, too, that during my six months in jail I had already developed a certain cynicism toward the administration of justice in our courts, a cynicism that had been confirmed that very day in that very same courtroom.

The judges who sentenced me to life imprisonment in the penal colonies of Guiana had, a few hours earlier, sentenced another man to ten years. This man had been found guilty of murdering his two-year-old son. He had beaten the child's brains out against a stone wall and dumped the tiny corpse into an open sewer. The court ruled that he had been temporarily insane at the time and it chose to be lenient. The rest of us in that jail wondered whether perhaps the fact that the murderer's name was prefaced by a title, *Monsieur le Vicomte,*

could have influenced the court in any way. The eminent
judges would most certainly have indignantly denied the
charge. Clearly, in their eyes, I was a far more dangerous
criminal and guilty of a much more serious crime than the
slaughter of a helpless baby. The sentence they had passed on
Monsieur le Vicomte did not make it difficult for me to meet
their gaze with no feeling of shame whatever. Later, in the
prison camp at St. Laurent, I had occasion to meet *Monsieur
le Vicomte.* He was universally detested and shunned by even
the most hardened convict in the camp. But convicts, as everyone knows, have a peculiar sense of justice.

I was glad to be leaving France. I was glad to be leaving
Marilyn and Joel and Delanoit and even Paulette. I was glad
to have reached the definitive ending of a long, peculiar chapter in my life. I was glad to be able to leave my own sense of
shame behind—not the shame I was supposed to feel before my
judges and society, but the shame I felt because I had betrayed
myself, because I had not lived up to my own best instincts as
an artist. In Guiana, perhaps, it would be different; I would
find the time to paint. And there was always the possibility of
escape.

This possibility was something we convicts thought about
and discussed constantly. Not one of us was resigned to spending the rest of his life in a jungle work camp. From the first,
we all dreamed and plotted escape, even those of us who had
only comparatively brief sentences to serve. Whatever actual
prison term a man had been sentenced to, the system of *doublage,* still very much in force, automatically doubled it. Freedom was something to be fought for, permanently available
only to those bold enough and enterprising enough to get
away.

During the long days of imprisonment in the grim island

fortress of St. Martin de Ré, off the town of La Rochelle in
northern France, while awaiting transfer to Guiana, we made
our plans, estimated our chances. There were several old hands
among us, men who had already served time in Guiana, and
they told us what to expect. The problem, we discovered, was
not so much the escape itself, which was feasible, but avoiding
eventual recapture. French Guiana is bounded on three sides
by almost impenetrable jungle and on the fourth by the open
sea. Escape to the south, toward Brazil, was impossible either
overland, because of the jungle, or by sea, because the prevail-
ing trade winds blow the wrong way and the Amazon current
pushes against you. Escape to the north depended entirely on
persuading the Dutch in Surinam not to hold you for extradition by the French authorities and the Dutch had by that time
acquired a reputation for being inhospitable to fugitives: they
always extradited them. Beyond the Dutch were the British,
who would allow you to rest among them for a week or so and
then would insist that you move on. Beyond the British were
the Venezuelans, who welcomed convicts with open arms and
set them right to work in chain gangs on local civic projects
such as roads and railways. The route directly into the interior,
through uncharted jungle, over unclimbed mountains, past the
territories of untamed Indian tribes, was equivalent to suicide.
The best route was by sea, through the Caribbean Islands to the
coast of Central America, but this meant finding a boat, sup-
plying it, organizing a crew, and braving the French and
Dutch coastal patrols.

None of these considerations and drawbacks in the least
dampened the enthusiasm with which we all awaited arrival
in Guiana. Some of the men even spoke of the place in much
the same way Columbus' sailors and Walter Raleigh's soldiers
must have referred to it, as a kind of promised land, an El

Dorado, in which anything and everything was possible. To understand this attitude, you have to remember that life in a mainland prison was extremely harsh and confined, with no freedom of physical movement and certainly no hope at all of escape. In Guiana, whatever happened, we would be outdoors a good deal of the time and benefiting from the open-air routine of camp life. A prison just the same, of course, but a prison without bars. As for the hazards of escape, there was not a man among us who did not feel that he would be the exception to the rule, that he would succeed where others had failed, that he alone was destined for eventual freedom in some island paradise or in the hospitable, humanitarian nations of North America. I was no different from anyone else and I looked forward to the day of departure from France with impatience.

On March 6, 1931, I was one of 900 silent men who shuffled single file through the watching streets of La Rochelle, along the bleak quay lined by spectators, friends, and weeping relatives, up the gangplank, and into the dismal interior of the prison ship *La Martinière*, an old captured German freighter that had once made the regular run between Hamburg and the Cameroons. Inside, we were herded into large cages, a hundred or a hundred and fifty men to a cage, and given hammocks to suspend from the bars in the ceiling. The cages were crowded, uncomfortable, and hot, and, with our shaved heads, our ill-fitting, striped prison costumes, our prison pallor, we looked like a sullen tribe of white apes. Outside the cages, our guards, aloof and disdainful, strolled the aisles in pairs, patrolling their private zoo.

I will not dwell in detail on the discomforts of that trip, because the third day out I managed to have myself transferred to the infirmary, where I was given a bed of my own and allowed the run of the ship. I had secured this privilege for my-

self by drawing sketches of the guards, all of whom turned out
to be infected with the normal amount of human vanity. The
sketches established me as something of a celebrity on board—
I was given all the paper and pencils I needed and soon I was
drawing pictures of all the ship's officers as well—and I was
freed from the general suffering below decks. Suffice it to say
that that suffering was extreme. The trip took fifteen days and
the men were brought on deck only once a day and for only
an hour at a time. The portholes were few and small and the
air was foul. Half the men were seasick and some of them lay
helplessly on the floor in their own vomit. Fights broke out and
to quell them the guards would turn fire hoses loose upon the
men, drenching the innocent and the guilty alike. The older,
more experienced convicts ganged up together and stole from
the weaker ones. Homosexuality, always a major problem in
prison life, flowered and the younger boys were soon, almost
without exception, forced to accept liaisons with one of *les
vieux*, as the old hands were called, if only for their own protection. My artistic skills had temporarily freed me from these
horrors and I was more than glad to have found a refuge from
them.

As I said, I was allowed the run of the boat and I took full
advantage of this privilege to make sketches for myself as well
as for others. No one was at all worried that I would make any
attempt to escape, since, as we came nearer to the coast of
South America, the sea began literally to teem with ominous
black fins following in our wake. Never before had I seen so
many sharks in one place and it wasn't likely that I would be
foolhardy enough to try to swim out through that pack of kill-
ers. I spent hours leaning on the rail, staring down at them in
fascination. Once, a guard joined me. He grinned and nudged
me with his elbow. "A pretty sight, eh, Lagrange?" he said.

"It's not unusual around here, you know. They follow every ship like that. Remember that sight when you get ready to escape, Lagrange. Oh, you'll try it. They all do. Just make sure your boat doesn't leak, eh, Lagrange? We train them to eat prisoners in Guiana. They're used to human flesh. Don't try to swim your way out, Lagrange. No one ever has."

Early one morning I was awakened by the insistent tooting of a siren. I went up on deck. There was a feeling of excitement in the air, a stirring in the cages below. From one of the portholes a voice shouted, "Land! Land!" Other voices took up the cry and there were curses and screams as men fought for positions at the tiny windows. On deck, guards were running back and forth, shouting to one another. The ship's engines had been cut and she bobbed gently in the slow offshore swell. The air was stifling and gulls wheeled above the masts. In the distance, hardly visible along the horizon, I could just make out the low-lying contours of a thick, wooded coast line. We had arrived at the broad mouth of the Maroni River, only a few hours from our destination of St. Laurent.

The siren I had heard belonged to a small motor launch that had come out from the shore to meet us. On board was a large group of prison officials, nattily dressed in spotless white uniforms and pith helmets. The launch was slowly drifting toward us, evidently preparing to transfer the officials to *La Martinière* before piloting us up the river. I was calmly surveying this scene from my usual post at the rail when one of the guards suddenly grabbed me. "My God, Lagrange!" he said, hustling me away. "Get the hell down below with the others! You're not supposed to be up here! Do you want the chief to see you when he comes on board? What kind of a prison ship do you think this is, anyway?"

So that was the end of my special privileges. For the remainder of the trip, until we finally docked at St. Laurent five hours later, I was forced to share the discomforts of my fellow convicts. However, I had learned a valuable lesson; my experience on board *La Martinière* had taught me that all convicts are equal in the eyes of the law but that some convicts, to paraphrase the English writer George Orwell, are more equal than others.

During the length of time it took us to navigate the river, we all took turns at the portholes and described what we saw to the rest of the men. Unfortunately, there really wasn't much to tell. The banks of the Maroni were distant, dark green, blurred in the haze of humidity that rose like steam from the river. Every now and then we'd see a rooftop or the flashing white of a wall and there would be a stir of excitement among us, but for the most part we felt ourselves more cut off than ever, alone in a vast and openly hostile jungle. A mood of depression settled over all of us in the cages. What awaited us at St. Laurent, the capital of the *bagne?* Was it merely a stockade, an open camp lost in the boundless wilderness? We had been told that it was a good-sized town, the seat of the penal administration, the location of the central penal colony, the site of the main reception depot. During these months we had come to think of St. Laurent as an end and a beginning. But now, staring out of the portholes at the distant shores of the Maroni, enveloped in silence, we began to have our doubts. Escape at that moment seemed an absolute impossibility.

At last the time came for us to gather up our prison sacks and file out of *La Martinière* into the tropical sunlight of our new world. Two by two, like the animals disembarking from the Ark, we walked down the gangplank and lined up along the length of a long wooden dock while the guards barked orders at us and called the roll. At the end of the pier a large crowd had collected to watch our arrival. There were prison officials and their wives, a few children, some wretched-looking men in rags (*libérés*, I found out later), and a gay, swarming mass of blacks, laughing and joking among themselves and calling out raucous greetings to us. Behind the crowd lay the town of St. Laurent, a state within a state.

Imagine our amazement, after all our doubts and fears, to find ourselves now confronted by a perfect jewel of a little city, a toy town almost out of a child's fairy tale, with spotless streets and bright, neat little houses, freshly painted, their windows alive with flower boxes, gay curtains, and wooden shutters! In every square, in every street, flowers bloomed; palm trees waved lazily in the breeze. From where we stood, mouths agape, on the pier, even our fellow convicts fitted perfectly into that dreamlike scene, their striped uniforms of red and white seeming as appropriate to the setting as if they had been donned expressly to enhance it. So this was the dreaded *bagne!* A great sigh of relief swept through our ranks.

After we had been counted, the guards divided us into groups of fifty or more and marched us off along the river bank. Eventually, about half a mile beyond the town, we turned left and entered a large walled camp through a gate over which was written: *"Camp de la Transportation."* This was the main reception depot. Here we would be sorted out and assigned to other areas. As soon as we had arrived, the guards dismissed us and we were allowed to shift for ourselves. The men rushed for the barracks and staked out their claims to personal living quarters, then gathered together in small knots of friends, smoked, traded valuables, and discussed the mysterious future. We were left alone until evening, when the shrill whistles of the guards summoned us out into the open to hear the commandant of St. Laurent make his traditional welcoming speech.

He was a short, heavy-set man with a thin mouth and a voice like a bronze clapper and he was evidently not delighted with our appearance. Surrounded by a tight-faced knot of his subordinates, he surveyed the ragged lines of our semi-military formation, placed his hands on his hips, and shouted: "You have been sent here to expiate your crimes. . . . Those of you who fail to understand your position will expiate doubly for your behavior. . . . Here there is only one formula: do your job or take the consequences. . . . Now, those of you who go along with us will, after a certain number of years, receive shortened sentences, but, even before obtaining such pardons as you may earn, you will also be able to enjoy certain small favors—better living conditions, canteen privileges, and so on —I repeat, there is only one discipline here and we'll enforce it. . . . Those of you who wish to go to the right, will go to the right. Those of you who wish to go to the left, will go to the left. . . . But never forget that the law is stronger than you are and that we are here to see that the law is obeyed. . . . And as for escape, forget about it! . . ."

I'm sorry to say that this impressive speech was received by most, if not all, of us with complete indifference. What influence could these absurd phrases have on men who had already served time in the brutal prisons of metropolitan France? At best, they could only confuse and cow the weaklings and mental defectives among us. We heard them out in derisive silence, after which we were dismissed for the night. Some of the men returned to their barracks, others made for the canteen. Our main preoccupation was with the morning, for it was then that we expected to receive our permanent assignments and begin our years of forced labor.

That day began with a medical examination, the main purpose of which was to determine our fitness to work. With that inbred cynicism common to convicts and old soldiers, we instinctively sensed that it was important not to be found in splendid physical condition, since a man capable of doing any sort of work would quite probably be sent to one of the jungle camps to fell trees or be put out in the sun to build roads. It was much more desirable to be esteemed fit for only the lightest sort of task, such as gathering leaves or raking up grass someone else had cut or picking up cigarette butts, preferably on the shady side of the street. There was one classification we all aspired to: the Incapables, men unable to work at all. Unfortunately, to qualify as an Incapable you had to be either blind or crippled. Naturally, we all did our best. Men with torsos like Greek statues showed up coughing and wheezing; purse snatchers and second-story men developed alarming limps; the roughnecks and bullies of the camp turned out to be as delicate as schoolgirls, hardly able to lean over to tie their own shoelaces. Admirable as these impersonations were, they almost never fooled the camp doctor, a veteran connoisseur of the malingerer's art. Ninety per cent of the men were judged fit and able to work at hard labor. They were immediately assigned to one or the other of the work camps.

I was one of the last to be examined and I had adequate time to study the situation. I was anxious to achieve one of two possible classifications, either to be found fit for only the lightest tasks or to be recognized as a person of special abilities, which would perhaps leave me some freedom of movement about the town and also make it possible for me to earn some money on the side. The question of money was, of course, crucial, since it was impossible in prison as in civilian life to exist without it. Money bought such clandestine luxuries as liquor and tobacco, favors from the guards, and, most important, the supplies necessary to attempt an escape. Like the

other convicts, I already had my own secret cache. Most of
the men kept their valuables in their so-called *plans*, supposi-
tories made of bone or some non-corrosive metal, but I hid my
money by sewing it into the linings of the few books I had
been allowed to bring with me from France. I was eager to
build up that cache, which then consisted of only a few hundred francs. It was absolutely essential, I realized as I stood
there in that long line of shuffling men, that I convince this
hard-nosed medical genius of my unique qualities.

At last my turn came. Rejoicing in my naturally slender,
somewhat emaciated physique, I stood naked before the great
doctor. He examined me perfunctorily, obviously unaware or
indifferent to the precarious state of my health. I did my best
to smother a cough. No reaction. The doctor took my blood
pressure, sighed, and scribbled something on a sheet of paper.

"All right, you, move on now."

"Doctor——"

"You're as healthy as a horse. Move along now."

"I am an artist, *Monsieur*. I would like some work that would
make use of my talent."

The doctor looked up from his sheet of paper and fixed me
with a malicious smile. "You would, eh?"

"Yes, sir."

"We'll get you started right away then."

"Yes, sir. I'm truly grateful, sir."

The doctor went to the door of his little office and summoned one of the guards. He laughed and waved in my direction. "Listen," he told the guard, "this man is an artist. He
wishes to go to work at once on a project that will make good
use of his talent. Tell him that I have just such a project. Give
him a broom and let's see how artistically he sweeps out my
waiting room."

The guard grinned and cocked a thumb at me. "All right, get your clothes on, Lagrange, and get busy."

My guess is that the waiting room had not been swept in several years. During that time generations of convicts in muddy or dusty boots had tramped back and forth across its cracked concrete surface. I labored like Hercules in the Augean stables, with the grim dedication of a desperate man. My future seemed desolate. I saw myself condemned to years of such work in one camp after another. Because I had lost hope and felt that I had nothing more to lose, I decided to amuse myself. Using my broom as an enormous brush, I began to draw caricatures in the dust at my feet. I populated the floor of the waiting room with the heads of my fellow convicts, the guards, even a portrait of my enemy the doctor himself. The caricatures were necessarily crude, but not entirely without merit. I became so engrossed in what I was doing that I didn't notice the entrance of the doctor, who had finished with his examinations and had dropped in to see how I was doing.

I don't know how long he had been standing there. I looked up, saw his feet in the doorway, and, without losing a stroke, I reconverted my brush into a broom and resumed my labors.

"Stop that," the doctor said.

I gazed up at him in angelic innocence. "I'm sorry, sir, did I——"

"What's your name again?"

"Lagrange, Francis Lagrange," I said glumly. "Convict Number Six Two Three——"

"Never mind all that," the doctor said. "Come in here. I'm going to give you a slip you're to take over to headquarters. They can use you over there. Can you paint as well as you draw?"

"Better."

"Good. I'm classifying you permanently for light work only. You'll be used for special decorative assignments. I'm sure they'll be glad to have someone like you around for these jobs." I opened my mouth to thank him. "Don't," he said impatiently. "I know you're as big a faker as the rest of them, but there's no sense trying to put *you* to work. I never met an artist yet who was worth a damn when it came to doing a man's job."

That doctor was clearly one of life's noblemen. I took the slip he wrote out for me directly over to prison headquarters and within half an hour I was ushered into the office of the director of the camp of St. Laurent itself. He was a stern-faced, elderly *gendarme* colonel named Maurice Frank.

Colonel Frank read through the doctor's note in silence, then leaned back in his chair and looked at me. "So you are an artist, Lagrange."

"Yes, sir."

"My friend the doctor seems to have a high opinion of your talent."

"Yes, sir."

"I respect my friend the doctor's opinions. You will be permanently assigned to this office and will execute whatever tasks I myself will set for you. We have a lot to do around here."

"Yes, sir. Thank you, sir."

"Don't get any ideas, Lagrange. You came here as a convict and you are going to be treated like any other convict." A pause. "Of course, being attached to this office, you'll be able to benefit in certain ways and you will enjoy certain privileges, privileges that can be revoked at any time. Is that clear?"

"Yes, sir."

"You're going to work and work hard. There's plenty to do around here, make no mistake." A pause. "You understand?"

"Perfectly, sir."

A well-organized escape along the Upper Maroni.

Colonel Frank picked up a large, framed photograph that was standing on his desk and handed it to me. It was a picture of a young, handsome woman holding a small, unpleasant-looking boy of four or five on her lap. "My wife and son," Colonel Frank said.

"My congratulations, sir." I handed the picture back to him.

Colonel Frank stood up, placed his hands behind his back, and gave me the full military treatment. "The first task you will execute, Lagrange, is to paint a portrait of my son. Any questions?"

What questions could there be? I took the easy road. "It will be a privilege, sir, and an honor."

Colonel Frank sat down again. "You will begin this afternoon," he said, dismissing me. "Report to my house at three o'clock. I will tell my wife to expect you."

I explained to Colonel Frank that it would be necessary for me to acquire paints, brushes, canvas, and other equipment before I could start work. The colonel nodded thoughtfully. "That seems reasonable enough," he said. "You can buy what you need in St. Laurent. How much will it cost?"

I told him that 200 francs would certainly cover everything, but that it might take me some time to find exactly what I wanted. "Take the afternoon, Lagrange, and report to my house at ten o'clock tomorrow morning." The colonel summoned an orderly, instructed him to provide me with a permanent pass for the town of St. Laurent and 200 francs from the administrative budget, and dismissed me. "Remember what I told you, Lagrange," he said sternly. "This is a prison, not a rest home."

By this time I knew pretty well what sort of a prison it was. I took my pass and my 200 francs, strolled nonchalantly back through the gates of the camp, and headed straight for the town.

The disciplinary prison courts had powers of life and death over us.

It was my first taste of freedom in nearly seven months and I reveled in it. I couldn't get away from the prison fast enough. By the time I reached the outskirts of the town itself I was almost running. On the way I passed a gnarled old convict lethargically at work trimming a hedge. He looked up and hailed me. "Hey," he said, "where the hell are you going?"

"Into town."

"What for?"

I told him and the old convict grinned and shook his head. "A painter, eh? Well, look at me, my friend. You see what I do here? I clip leaves all day. A snip here, a snip there. That's not so bad, is it?"

"Not bad at all."

"That's the trick, to find something that's not so bad," the old man said. "Now you, you look like you have enough sense to understand that."

"I do, I do."

"Then," the old man said, "then you'd better have the sense to slow down a bit. No matter what you do here, my friend, never do it in a hurry. Take your time, do it slowly. That's the best way to get along around here. Adopt the colonial pace, my friend, and you'll get along all right."

"The colonial pace?"

The old man nodded. "Yes. Never run if you can walk, never walk if you can stand, never stand if you can sit, never sit if you can lie down, and never do anything today you can put off until tomorrow. That's the colonial pace. Master it and things won't be so bad."

I immediately took the old man's advice. Sauntering idly through the neat, narrow streets of St. Laurent, I stopped in at a bar and bought myself a beer. Then I sat down in the shade of a doorway and surveyed the lethargic activity of the streets. After that, I had a short nap. After the nap, I strolled around some more and smoked a few cigarettes. Finally, when I could think of no other way to waste time, I stopped in at a general store and ordered the supplies I needed for my work. I arranged to stop by later and pick everything up. I still had an hour or so left before I had to return to the camp, so I decided to do some more sightseeing.

My wanderings through the town eventually brought me to the so-called Chinese Quarter, a slang phrase meaning the poorest section of a city. Here the town made no pretensions to civic virtue. Ugly old houses were crowded in upon one another, garbage littered the streets, dead rats floated in the open sewers, the stench of rot and poverty filled the air. Flocks of vultures gorged themselves on ordure, and the ragged, filthy children of the Quarter gamboled through them as if they were pigeons. From doorways and windows the incurious faces of the poor stared out at their own misery. The faces were mostly *Créole*, with here and there the pure-black features of a bush Negro or the flat, Eskimo-like cast of an Indian. There were also quite a few old whites, ancient derelicts with yellowing, rheumy eyes, unshaven cheeks, discolored teeth, and matted, lousy hair—the *libérés*, the victims of *doublage*, the permanent colonists on whom France had hoped to found the prosperity of her South American empire.

The Chinese Quarter of St. Laurent occupied a section of the waterfront, stretching for a mile or so above the pier where we had disembarked the day before. From where I now stood on the muddy, foul-smelling bank of the river I could see *La Martinière* at her berth; downstream from me a group of nearly naked bush Negroes were busily at work around the long, low shapes of their dugout canoes, the famous pirogues of South America. The mist that had obscured the river the day before had lifted and I could now clearly make out the opposite bank of the Maroni. I could see the clustered houses of a small, delightful-looking village nestled among the trees. I knew, from having studied the maps of the region, that it was probably the Dutch town of Albina. I stared at it hungrily, knowing that the land I was gazing upon was not French, knowing that that land represented freedom.

Not far from me, someone else was staring across the river, an old, defeated-looking white man dressed in dirty trousers and a frayed shirt. I guessed that he was probably one of the *libérés*, though he seemed in better condition than most of the others. He was sitting on the bank, smoking and occasionally muttering softly to himself. I walked over to him.

"What town is that?" I asked, pointing at the opposite bank.

"Albina," the man said, not taking his eyes from it.

"Is there any way to get there?"

"Getting there is easy," the man said. "Staying there is another matter."

"How can I get there?"

The man waved in the direction of the bush Negroes and their pirogues. "Any one of them will take you across, for a price."

"How much?"

"A hundred francs."

I still had all of the money that had been given to me to pay for my supplies and I started at once for the pirogues. "Wait a minute!" the man called out in back of me. "You can't go over there just like that! They'll send you back right away! I've tried it a dozen times myself!"

I was not going to listen to him. I had made up my mind. Good-by, St. Laurent! Good-by, fellow convicts! Good-by, my kind doctor and Colonel Frank and my commandant with the voice like a bronze clapper! Good-by, French Guiana! Good-by, prison life! Good-by, good-by, good-by!

Twenty minutes later I was stretched out on the bottom of a long pirogue, being paddled across the majestic Maroni by two muscular blacks. I had served not quite thirty-six hours of my life sentence at hard labor in the penal colonies of the *bagne*.

12 Dutch Treat

IT was nearly dark when I stepped ashore from my pirogue and shook the hands of my deliverers, who at once turned their boat around and began the return trip to St. Laurent. I could still just barely make out the contours of the French shore line, along which the lights of evening now winked as if to compliment me on my rapid escape. I could hardly believe that I was actually free, out so quickly from under the heel of the French penal system. However, I had no time to congratulate myself. The pirogue had landed me only a few hundred yards below the town of Albina. I knew that in a matter of minutes one of the shore patrols would find me and I had to be prepared. With the rest of my francs I had bought a shabby suit of clothes from one of my crew and I now hastily ripped off my prison uniform, rolled it up, buried it in the mud of the river bank, and donned my new outfit. Not a moment too soon. I had hardly finished buttoning up my shirt when a harsh, guttural voice spun me around.

"You, fat are you doing dere? Fat are you?"

The voice was speaking reasonably accurate French, but the pronunciation was unmistakable. Until that instant I hadn't had any idea what I would do or say when confronted by the

Dutch police, but that voice had given me my cue. I affected
an air of nonchalance and walked forward a few steps, hoping
to locate the owner of it. "Good evening," I said in German.
A man stepped out of the shadows. He was dressed in a
police uniform and was holding a rifle pointed at my belly. He
chose to ignore my salutation in German and continued to
speak French. "Fell? Answer or I shoot. You are a confict, no?"
Again I answered in German. "No, no, my dear sir," I said,
smiling, "I'm not a convict. Nor a *libéré*. I've come here to
visit Albina and I'd be very grateful if you'd take me to your
superior."
The man peered at me through the gloom and lowered his
rifle a few inches. "You're a German?" he asked, speaking his
own native language at last.
"Yes. That upsets you?"
He lowered the rifle all the way and came up to me. "Oh,
no, on the contrary, I'm extremely happy to meet a country-
man. But what were you doing in St. Laurent?"
"I was there on business."
"Business?"
"Semi-political business," I said, trying to sound mysterious.
"Ah, so," the man said, nodding as if what I had told him
explained anything at all. "Come along then."
He took me at once back to the central police station of
Albina and ushered me into the small, barren office of his
superior. Behind a gleaming desk sat an absolutely typical
German face, young-looking, pink, unlined, with snapping
blue eyes and very short, bristling blond hair. The face took
me in at a glance as I entered the room and, before I could
utter a word, addressed me in French in much the same tone
used by my escort. "Fat are you doing here?"
I gazed into those sharp, very blue eyes and I realized at

once that the explanation I had improvised on the river bank
would not do. I decided to risk at least a portion of the truth,
but I continued to speak German. "Yes," I said, "I am a convict and I've just escaped from St. Laurent."

The blue eyes opened wide in surprise. "You speak German?
You are German?"

"Yes."

A slow, malicious smile spread over the Teutonic features
of my interrogator. "From what part of Germany?"

"Hamburg."

"Hamburg? You are from Hamburg?" the man said, amazed.
He pushed his chair back, stood up, leaned both hands on his
desk, and shouted at me: "Hummel!"

I laughed. "Kiss my ass!" I shouted back.

An uninitiated onlooker might have expected the German
at this point to strike me or take some other form of drastic
action. He certainly would have been astounded at the reaction my words actually caused. The police officer threw back
his head and roared with glee, then came around the desk and
embraced me. "My God," he said, "we're from the same home
town!"

The explanation of this curious exchange is very simple.
Toward the end of the last century, there lived in Hamburg
an old hunchback named Hummel, who sold drinking water
through the streets of the town. Every day his gnarled, stooped
form could be seen plodding from door to door, a long pole
with buckets attached slung over his shoulders. Everywhere
he went he was always followed by gangs of jeering children
who danced after him, gleefully shouting his name over and
over: "Hummel! Hummel!" And the old hunchback always
answered in the same way: "Kiss my ass, kiss my ass!" Eventually, this exchange became incorporated into the daily life

of the town. People shouted "Hummel" at total strangers and, if they received the traditional answer, knew that the strangers were not strangers at all, but citizens of Hamburg. Today, all over the world, when Hamburgers wish to locate fellow citizens among crowds of strangers, they will cry, "Hummel, Hummel!" And if someone answers, "Kiss my ass!" they know they are among friends. I had lived in Hamburg for a total of eight years, off and on, I spoke German with the accent of a genuine Hamburger, and now, in these odd surroundings and circumstances, fate had put me into the hands of a homesick fellow citizen. Evidently my luck had changed and I was riding a winning streak.

The police officer instructed me to call him by his first name, Max, and insisted that I come home with him to meet his wife, a fat, jolly Dutch girl he had met and married in Albina. Settled comfortably in his living room, Max asked me how I happened to wind up in the *bagne*. I improvised brilliantly. My name was Hans Bergen, I told him. I was an artist, I had lived in France for many years and had been interned there during the war. After the war, the French had repatriated me as an undesirable alien. "What could I do?" I said helplessly. "I am an artist, Max, and Paris was and is still the capital of the art world. Of course I wanted to go back there. So I went back with false identity papers. I lived there for nearly six years before I was caught. The French accused me of being a spy and sentenced me to life imprisonment."

Max was outraged. "Life imprisonment? Incredible!"

I shrugged philosophically. "Well, you know how the French feel about us Germans. What could I do?"

Max paced angrily up and down the room. "The damn French," he said, "that's the way it's always been with them. And they wonder why we Germans have to teach them a lesson every twenty years!" He stopped his agitated pacing and looked at me compassionately. "But what about you now, Hans? What will you do?"

"Well, naturally," I said, "I'd like to get home."

Max slammed his hands together. "By God, of course you'll get home!" he said. "Today is Monday and the steamer for Paramaribo arrives on Thursday. From there you'll be able to arrange passage back to Germany. Do you have any money?"

"No, I'm afraid not."

"I'll loan you some. You can repay me when you get home."

"You're very kind, Max."

"Kind?" Max came over to me and put his hands on my shoulders. "Kind? Wouldn't you do the same for a fellow citizen?"

With tears in my eyes, I confessed that I would.

"Tell me, Max," I said later, over our fifth beer, "how does it happen that so many of you in the Dutch police seem to be German?"

"We lost the war," Max said emotionally. "For many of us there was nothing to do in Germany. We had to go abroad, you know. Well, here we are in Surinam. There are several hundred of us stationed here. The Dutch couldn't get their own men to serve in this God-forsaken place, so we Germans fill the void. But some day, Hans, some day we'll all go back to Germany, won't we? Yes, some day we'll show the world what it means to be a German!"

I spent a good part of the next two days strolling along the Albina waterfront, staring across the Maroni at the distant houses of St. Laurent. I couldn't take my eyes off the place. Was I really going to get away as easily as all that? Somehow I couldn't quite believe in my luck and I watched the river anxiously for any signs of a French boat. To distract myself

I spent some of the money Max had loaned me on a sketch pad and pencils; I drew portraits of the men in Max's post, of the colorfully dressed citizens of Albina, of the mayor himself. By Thursday morning, when the *Princess Juliana,* the small coastal steamer making the regular run to Paramaribo, arrived, I had become a celebrity. Everyone in Albina knew that I was that German artist who had escaped from St. Laurent and was going home to Hamburg.

Max himself accompanied me on board the boat. We had had several farewell beers together and we marched down the pier, arm in arm, singing songs of old Hamburg. Max had a powerful off-pitch baritone. "Toward our Fatherland we are marching," we sang, the words floating defiantly across the water to the shores of Guiana. It was all Max could do to part from me. But at last, after several emotional embraces, he ran down the gangplank, the *Princess Juliana* tooted her horn three times, and we moved out into the middle of the stream. We made a wide circle, skirting quite close to the French shore. I leaned against the railing, watching St. Laurent slide past. Several people on the river bank waved at us and I waved back. "Good-by, St. Laurent," I said with a deep sigh of relief, "nevermore, nevermore!"

My elation was a little premature. Nothing happened on the two-day boat trip to shake my confidence (I made myself popular with the captain by executing a portrait of his wife from a photograph he kept in his cabin), but when the *Princess Juliana* docked at Paramaribo, the capital of Surinam, a tall, elegant, austere young man in an impeccable white uniform presented himself to me, clicking his heels together and nodding curtly. "Kleinhod," he said, "chief of police of Paramaribo. Follow me, please."

He escorted me through the crowd of curious onlookers on

the dock, into his automobile, and we drove directly to police headquarters. There I was shown into his office, the door closed behind us, and we sat down facing each other. "All right," Kleinhod said, wasting no time on preliminaries. "Who are you?"

I hesitated several seconds before answering. What should I tell him? The truth? Kleinhod was also quite obviously a German or of German descent. However, I realized at once that I was not dealing with another Max, but with a highly trained, unemotional professional, a man who would place his duty above his personal feelings. His manner to me had been absolutely correct, but distant and precise. I was face to face with a career officer of the highest type (I found out later that he was a graduate of the police academy of New York) and I knew I wasn't going to get anywhere by appealing to his emotions.

Nevertheless, I realized that I could hardly tell him the truth. It was a well-known fact that the Dutch always repatriated all French fugitives from justice. For many years now there had been no exceptions to this rule and I had nothing to gain by admitting the truth. I decided to persist in my bluff and to confirm the story Chief Kleinhod must have already heard by telegraph from Max. I was indeed Hans Bergen, I said, and I repeated my improvised tale.

Kleinhod heard me out in silence, betraying no emotion whatever, then indicated a table with a typewriter and some blank sheets of paper on it. "All right, *Herr* Bergen," he said, "you will now write down for me your complete *curriculum vitae*, right up to your arrival in Paramaribo. I want facts, dates, and places. Please omit nothing. You will include a complete family history, addresses and so on."

The assignment did not dismay me, because I had an ace

or two up my sleeve. I knew Hamburg like the back of my hand and it wasn't hard to concoct an account of my life that could be checked out, at least on the surface. After all, it wasn't too unnatural for me to put down that both my parents were dead and that I had no other living relatives. As for the name of Hans Bergen, I had not simply plucked it out of the air. During my years in Hamburg, I had used this name as a political cartoonist for a satirical weekly and I had become quite famous under it, to the point that I had often introduced myself and been known as Hans Bergen. I felt reasonably confident that a merely routine check would confirm my German identity and succeed in getting me out of Surinam. In any case, it was the only chance I had and I took it.

When I had finished and Chief Kleinhod had read through my account in silence, he took me to see the German consul in Surinam, a certain Dr. Halsmann. The consul also read through my *curriculum vitae*, nodding heavily from time to time, and then informed me that if the story were true I would be repatriated to Germany. It was the policy of the German Government, he said, to aid all nationals victimized by French injustice. However, until the matter had been gone into more thoroughly, I would remain in Paramaribo as a guest of the Dutch administration. It would take a few weeks for the necessary check to be concluded; Dr. Halsmann hoped that I would not object to waiting. Chief Kleinhod would make all the proper arrangements. I said that of course I would not mind waiting, that I understood the situation perfectly, and that I was ever at Chief Kleinhod's disposal.

For the next three weeks I was dressed, fed, and housed in Paramaribo at the expense of the Dutch Government. I enjoyed complete freedom to wander about the town, though I was required to check in daily at Chief Kleinhod's office. In addition, I received three florins a day for spending money. Of course, to a man of my extravagant tastes this was hardly sufficient, but it wasn't long before I was drawing and painting portraits of various prominent citizens and being well-recompensed for them. Paramaribo was a much larger and more worldly town than St. Laurent and I soon recaptured some of the flavor of my Paris life. Since I was still bleeding from Marilyn, I avoided women, except on an extremely casual basis. Still, my life was pleasant, the future reasonably promising, and I felt more confident as each day passed that I had escaped for good.

One day, when I showed up to check in at the police station, Chief Kleinhod sent for me. "*Herr* Bergen, I believe you speak French?" I nodded. "Then please follow me."

He took me back through the station toward the detention cells. There I was suddenly brought face to face with six desperate-looking men in a pitiable condition. They were in rags, covered with sores and parasites, emaciated, feverish, their eyes peering wildly out from behind matted hair and tangled beards. Despite their terrible state, I immediately recognized two of the men who had come over with me on *La Martinière*. What was worse, I knew that they had instantly recognized me, despite my healthy appearance and civilian clothes. We stared at each other, my heart freezing.

"These men were picked up yesterday in the bush," Chief Kleinhod said. "They're fugitives like yourself. Our interpreter is unfortunately ill and I must interrogate them. My French is not what it should be. Will you translate for me, *Herr* Bergen?"

Could I refuse? For the next fifteen or twenty minutes I acted as interpreter for Chief Kleinhod. The men answered briefly and to the point. To my relief I was not betrayed, but the two who knew me never took their eyes from me. After the interrogation had been concluded and Chief Kleinhod had started to walk away, one of them came up to the bars of the cell and clutched at my sleeve. "Lagrange," he whispered, "what are you doing here? Are you working for the police?" I had no time to do anything but wink at him and make a gesture with one hand, urging him to be silent; then I followed Chief Kleinhod.

"Poor devils," I said to him as we parted. "They must have had a rough time of it."

Kleinhod looked at me expressionlessly. "Every year gangs of men try to get out behind us through the bush," he said. "They never make it. If the jungle doesn't get them, we do." I turned to go. "By the way, *Herr* Bergen, what did that man say to you on the way out?"

"Nothing important," I said. "He wanted to know what would happen to them."

"They'll be sent back, of course," Kleinhod said. "In a week or two, after we fatten them up a bit."

To this day I'm not quite sure what happened. The only certainty is that sometime during the ensuing week, while the fugitives were waiting to be sent back to St. Laurent my real identity was revealed to the Dutch authorities. Perhaps those wretched men were jealous of my good fortune, perhaps they thought I had become a police spy. I don't know. I prefer to think it was an accident, but who knows what is hidden in the hearts of men?

Whatever the reason, I was not immediately aware of the change in my status. I continued to live comfortably in Paramaribo, though I did notice that it seemed to be taking a very long time to hear from Germany. When I finally went to see Dr. Halsmann some weeks later, he was evasive in his answers. Finally, after two months had passed, I was once more called into Chief Kleinhod's office.

He was sitting behind his broad desk, shuffling through some papers, and he seemed more expansive than usual as he indicated that I should sit down opposite him. "Well," he said, looking at me with a strange half-smile on his face, "you really are to be complimented."

"Indeed?" I answered. "For what?"

"You almost fooled me, Lagrange. Almost, but not quite."

I was too crushed to answer. Kleinhod continued: "Don't you want to know how we found out?"

I shrugged. "What difference does it make?"

Chief Kleinhod offered me a cigarette and even leaned over his desk to light it for me. "I'm sorry, Lagrange," he said. "I really am. I don't suppose you'll believe me, but I really was hoping that your story would check out. As it is, I have no alternative but to send you back. You do understand?"

"I understand."

He tapped the papers on his desk. "A very fascinating dossier," he said. "In view of your extraordinary reputation in the field of high finance, I hope you won't mind if I feel compelled to escort you back to St. Laurent in person."

"I don't mind."

"Good." Chief Kleinhod stuck out his hand and I shook it, without much enthusiasm, I must confess. "Nice try, Lagrange," he said. "Nothing personal, you know."

13 Monsieur Tronoir

I HAD found my two-month stay in Surinam more than pleasant and I was sorry to have to leave. I had entered actively into the professional and social life of the town and had won some renown for myself, both as an artist and because of the aura of romance that automatically surrounded anyone who had actually managed to escape from the *bagne*. Also, modesty aside, I've always been able to get along in any kind of society. To the stolid, humorless Dutch burghers of Paramaribo I was a mysterious and attractive figure and I was soon in much demand even in the best households of the city. I've always enjoyed a good party, I love company, and I accepted every invitation.

One of my greatest admirers was a short, nervous little man named Hugo Monk. He was a high-ranking civilian officer of the police administration, second only to Chief Kleinhod himself, and though I never knew exactly what his job was, I was certain that he was excellent at it. He had a genius for figures and was the sort of man who would see the stickiest assignment through under any conditions—an invaluable type to have around any kind of bureaucratic establishment. I don't know why he was attracted to me, unless it was because we were absolute opposites, but he couldn't get enough of me. I was a frequent guest at his house, where I regaled him with wild stories, mostly invented, of my youthful Hamburg days, and I painted portraits of him, his wife, and his children, which he hung all over his house. I liked him well enough and I was naturally anxious to stay on his good side.

One day he summoned me into his office and asked me to sit down. He was nervous and seemed upset. "Hans," he said, "I don't know what to do. You've got to help me."

"Of course, Hugo, if I can."

"We've already made all the arrangements for the reception, but I'm sure we should have a speech and no one knows what to say. You see, in honor of our guest, it really should be delivered in French and we don't have anyone in the lodge who speaks French that well. Do you think you could help us out?"

"I'm a little confused," I said. "Perhaps if you start from the beginning. . . ."

Hugo Monk then explained that he was a Freemason and quite high up in his order. He and the other members of his lodge had arranged some welcoming festivities for a visiting fellow Freemason, a certain *Monsieur* Philippe Tronoir from French Guiana. Hugo was very anxious for everything to go off well because *Monsieur* Tronoir was not only an eminent lodge member but a high civilian dignitary of the French penal administration. In fact, he was a judge of the Special Maritime Tribunal, the court charged with judging and passing sentence on French convicts accused of crimes committed during their stay in Guiana. It was extremely important to Hugo Monk that *Monsieur* Tronoir, whom he had had the pleasure of meeting once in Cayenne, be received with appropriate pomp and the most delicate courtesy. It would not do for the welcoming address, for instance, to be delivered in garbled French.

Monsieur Tronoir spoke only his native language and would be offended if it turned out that the lodge members of Paramaribo could not even greet him in his own tongue. Would I, as a special favor to the lodge, write and deliver this address at the reception ceremony, Hugo wanted to know? And would I see to it that *Monsieur* Tronoir understood everything that was being done for him and enjoyed himself thoroughly?

As usual, I was in no position to refuse. I told Hugo that I would most certainly oblige and I went home to draft my welcoming speech. *Monsieur* Tronoir was scheduled to arrive the following morning and there was no time to be lost.

The next day we all went down to the boat to meet him. A band played Dutch and French martial airs and, as the flags of our two nations flapped in the breeze, Hugo Monk, the other members of the welcoming committee, and I mounted the temporary dais erected for the occasion. A large crowd, attracted by the music, had gathered and began to wave and cheer as the *Princess Juliana* neared the dock. Hugo Monk and the members of the committee were very nervous. As the passengers descended the gangplank, Hugo nudged me repeatedly. "Be careful," he said, "don't do anything until I give you the signal. You're sure you have the speech?" I patted my pocket. "Good, good," Hugo said. "Now watch me, do what I tell you."

At last *Monsieur* Tronoir appeared at the head of the gangplank. Hugo hurled himself over the edge of the platform and signaled frantically to the bandmaster. "Now, now!" he hissed.

The band struck up a deafening if somewhat ragged version of the *Marseillaise* and *Monsieur* Tronoir began majestically to descend the gangplank. In keeping with the French meaning of his name, he was one of the blackest men I had ever seen. He was short, chunky, with calm, aristocratic features and closely cropped gray hair, and he carried himself with awesome dignity. Seeing him make that unsmiling, deliberate, majestic descent from the steamer, I began to experience a twitch or two of nerves myself. Hugo, I am sorry to say, was a wreck. In attempting to go and escort *Monsieur* Tronoir personally to the dais, he tripped and fell down the stairs. He had to be rescued and dusted off, and someone else led *Monsieur* Tronoir to the spot where I and the other members of the welcoming committee awaited him.

The band was abruptly extinguished in mid-cacophony and I produced my speech. A hush settled over the crowd. Hugo, grinning idiotically, trembled at my side. *Monsieur* Tronoir, gleaming impassively in the morning sunlight, gazed with mild interest at me and waited. I rose to the occasion:

"It is with a feeling of deep gratitude and affection that to-day we welcome to Paramaribo a distinguished colleague, an honored brother, and a citizen of that great nation to which the world owes so much. It is with full hearts that we stand here today and extend the hand of friendship and the clasp of brotherly love to Philippe Tronoir. During this memorable day that he will spend among us as the guest of our lodge, our city, and our state, let us not forget that he is more than merely a guest, that he is a member of our Great Family. Let us gather him to our bosoms and let him bask in the warmth of our affection. Let us realize the honor that Philippe Tronoir does us by condescending to give of his valuable time in order to come here today. Let us acknowledge this honor by letting Philippe Tronoir see what sort of friends he has in Surinam. And so, our beloved brother, we welcome you to Surinam, we welcome you to Paramaribo, we welcome you to the lodge, we welcome you to our hearts. . . ."

There was a good deal more of this sort of thing. When I

had finished, Hugo Monk had tears in his eyes, and a cheer went up from the listening crowd. *Monsieur* Tronoir, melted by my eloquence, clasped me in his arms.

The rest of the day I never left his side. We toured the city, inspected the various administrative buildings, including the courts, and gathered at the lodge that evening for a splendid banquet. Nothing happened to mar the events, not even when Hugo managed to spill soup over himself, and at the end of the day, before returning on board the *Princess Juliana*, *Monsieur* Tronoir again embraced me. "*Mon cher* Hans," he said emotionally, "how can I ever thank you? If you are ever in Guiana, please don't hesitate to look me up. I shall be offended if you do not. Remember, *cher* Hans, I am ever at your disposal!"

My prominent role during these festivities may give some idea of the standing I had achieved in Paramaribo society during my stay there. As in Albina, I had become a celebrity, a role I have never been averse to, and I played it to the hilt. And even when it became known who I really was, the friends I had made did not desert me. Hugo Monk himself was among the large group of sorrowing acquaintances who came to the boat to see me off on the morning that Chief Kleinhod and I embarked for the return to St. Laurent. Furthermore, his later intervention with the French authorities after my return probably helped in securing me the most lenient treatment. As for *Monsieur* Tronoir, he was never to be at my disposal, but I was soon to be at his, under circumstances neither of us had anticipated.

14 *The Bagne*

CHIEF Kleinhod and I arrived in St. Laurent on a particularly brilliant morning in early June. Since we were both dressed in civilian clothes, we did not attract much attention. I was carrying a couple of heavy suitcases full of the belongings I had acquired in Surinam and no sooner had we stepped ashore than a couple of ragged-looking *libérés* relieved me of them, inquiring respectfully where we were bound for. I was too depressed to tell them, so I just waved in the vague general direction of the camp and we started off. When we came to the main gate and it became evident that the camp was our destination, the *libérés* shot us a look of utter contempt, dropped my bags, and hurried off without even waiting for their tip. Chief Kleinhod and I entered and presented ourselves at the main reception office just inside the gate.

We were received with the utmost courtesy and respect by the little functionary who sat behind the only desk in the room. He quite naturally took us both for visiting dignitaries of some sort and his manner was nothing short of obsequious. I had spent so little time in St. Laurent that I was all but unknown, except to the prisoners who had come over with me on *La Martinière,* the doctor, and Colonel Frank. "In what

way can I be of service to you gentlemen?" the little functionary inquired, smiling agreeably.

Chief Kleinhod spoke up in his halting French. "Have you
a record here of an escaped convict named Lagrange?" he
asked.

"Lagrange? Lagrange? Oh, yes," the little man said. "We
must have his record about somewhere. One moment, please."
He summoned an orderly and instructed him to locate my file,
then turned back to us. "And what about this Lagrange?"

"Where is he?" Kleinhod asked.

The man shrugged. "Who knows?" he said. "He escaped
two months ago. He's probably cruising about the Caribbean.
Why?"

Kleinhod indicated me. "Is this the man?" he asked.

The functionary's jaw dropped an inch or two and he stared
at me, speechless. "Him?" he said at last. "How should I know?
We'll find out. Wait a minute! I'll get his fingerprints taken
and then we can compare them and——" He began to shout
orders in all directions.

"Never mind, never mind," I said quietly. "I am Francis
Lagrange."

The little functionary sat down heavily behind his desk and
shook his head. "Well, I'll be damned!" was all he could manage to say.

Comical as this scene now seems to me in retrospect, I confess that it was anything but comical to me at the time. I had
had too sharp and complete a taste of freedom to resign myself
so quickly again to my fate. However, as I've indicated before,
I have the sort of temperament that makes rapid adjustments
to the vicissitudes of life and, though I was unhappy to be
back in St. Laurent, I was by no means in despair. My primary
concern, I recall, was to be reabsorbed into the life of the penal

colony without being too severely punished for my escape, since freedom is also a relative thing. If I couldn't have Paramaribo, I could perhaps have the best of St. Laurent. I realized, of course, that I had one important consideration going in my favor: my quick escape had been made possible by the privileged situation Colonel Frank had created for me, a situation he had had no right to create. I could hardly be severely punished without some aspect of that punishment reflecting badly on Colonel Frank himself.

That night, once again attired in prison costume, I slept in a locked cell. The next morning I went up before Colonel Frank, an interview I was certainly not looking forward to. In fact, standing at attention before his desk, I confess that my knees were more than a bit wobbly. Confronted by that stern visage, all the comforting rationalizations of the day before evaporated in smoke. I would not have been surprised if Colonel Frank had ordered me to be crucified and abandoned to the ants.

The good colonel allowed me to suffer in silence for a minute or two, then he leaned back in his chair and put his hands on his hips. His voice when he spoke was hard and cold. "Well, Rembrandt," he said, "you couldn't wait to know Guiana a little better before rushing off like that?" When I didn't answer, he stood up and put his hands behind his back. "All right, Lagrange, you got away with it this time. You'll have to go up before the Tribunal and, under ordinary circumstances, you'd be sent to the islands. You know that?"

"Yes, sir."

"However, I've already spoken to the court about you and I think they will let you off this once," he continued. "It won't work twice, I warn you. You can keep that in mind."

"Yes, sir."

"You'll appear before the court in a day or two. Until then you'll remain in your cell. Any questions?"

"No, sir."

"After your trial, you'll report directly to me."

"Yes, sir."

"And bring your brushes, Lagrange. My wife is still waiting." He turned his back on me. "You may go."

Actually, I was never formally brought to trial. Instead, a few days later, I was summoned into the private office of one of the judges. By that time I was confident that nothing more serious awaited me than a severe lecture and I went almost jauntily to the encounter. Imagine my horror when the door closed behind me and I found myself face to face with none other than *Monsieur* Philippe Tronoir!

The horror was mutual. *Monsieur* Tronoir stared at me in stupefaction, then leaped to his feet. "What!" he shrieked. *"You? You* are Francis Lagrange?"

I started to explain, but *Monsieur* Tronoir would have none of it. "My God," he said, "and to think that I embraced you in public in front of all those people! Why, I'll never be able to go to Paramaribo again! What must they think of me! I must have been mad! And as for you, I'll show you what it means to make a mockery of the French magistracy! I'll teach you a thing or two! No one's going to make a fool out of me! Oh, no, my fine fellow! You'll rot in solitary for this! I'll double your time! Now get out!"

And before I could say another word in my defense I was taken out of *Monsieur* Tronoir's office and put back into my little cell. I never expected to be let out of it again.

As in the case of my betrayal in Paramaribo, I'm not sure exactly what happened, what forces conspired to make *Monsieur* Tronoir relent. I do know that shortly after my return

Hugo Monk wrote a letter to him on my behalf and perhaps it arrived at the crucial psychological moment. Or perhaps, once he had cooled off, he was himself entertained by the preposterousness of the situation. In any case, whatever the reason, I was at last released, after nearly a week in solitary, and dispatched back to the jurisdiction of Colonel Frank. I never had another conversation with *Monsieur* Philippe Tronoir, but I did pass him from time to time in the streets of St. Laurent. On those occasions I always nodded respectfully to him as he marched majestically past, totally indifferent to my existence.

My life in St. Laurent during those early months of my imprisonment was not difficult. I executed my assigned tasks, kept to myself, maintained good relations with most of my fellow prisoners, and plotted escape. The prospect of escape was the one hope we prisoners could never abandon, no matter what our individual circumstances were. It was what kept us alive and going; without it we could not have borne our lot. This was as true of me as of anyone else, despite the fact that my life, compared to that of most of the other convicts, was easy.

I don't mean to imply that the convicts as a whole were badly treated. A great many lies and exaggerations have been written about the *bagne*, even by people who have served time in its camps and prisons. It's not hard to understand why. It's always more lucrative to paint the blackest and most sensational picture imaginable, because the bigger the scandal, the more appalling the atrocity, the greater will be the interest aroused on the part of the general public. Yes, there were scandals, there were atrocities, there was cruelty and injustice and violence, men suffered and died—all this is true. But these things were the exception, not the rule. It was not the policy of the French Government to dispatch prisoners to Guiana in order to torture and kill them, as has been asserted over and over in books and newspaper articles without end. When the injustices and atrocities were uncovered, the penal administration usually made every effort to correct them. In discussing the *bagne* it is important to remember that it was a penal colony, not a summer camp, that the faults and the injustices were and almost certainly are common to every other prison system in every corner of the earth. Some prisons are better than others, of course, but every prison bears its load of cruelty and shame and oppression. The *bagne* of French Guiana was no worse than most prisons and in some important respects considerably better. There was indeed one period during my years in the *bagne* that was truly dreadful, but it was created by the special circumstances of the French defeat during World War II and I will deal with it more fully later. In this little essay, I am only attempting to give a fair picture of the prison as it was during most of the time I spent in it.

Of every one hundred men sent to the *bagne*, about twenty-five did their assigned tasks, went about their business, and got along without too much difficulty; about twenty-five were partly or totally incapacitated, either because of age, mental condition, or illness; about twenty-five were under special disciplinary detention, either in St. Laurent itself, the jungle work camps around St. Jean, or on the islands; and about twenty-five were missing, having escaped or being in the process of escaping. The men who really suffered were those who, for one reason or another, refused to work or were persistently guilty of flouting the penal authority. A surprisingly large number of men would do no work of any kind and they were mostly kept under lock and key in one of several heavily guarded prisons. They were not abused, but their life was extremely hard, since in the equatorial climate of French Guiana the worst possible torture is to be kept indoors in close confinement for long periods of time. However, it was a condition of prison life that these men had imposed on themselves; they could have bettered their lot at any time by merely consenting to work.

The so-called *incos*, the incorrigibles, were those who received the worst treatment. For one thing, they were most exposed to violence from the guards, since they were always under the closest supervision, either in solitary confinement or at the hardest kind of work in the jungle camps. They were the toughest and most desperate men in the *bagne*, always up before the Special Maritime Tribunal for one offense or another. In all fairness, nothing, not even murder, can justify the methods used to discipline these men, especially the often gratuitous brutality of the guards, but again it is important to remember that the situation of the *incos* was largely of their own making. It is absurd to pretend indignation at the abuses of an entire system that is itself an abuse. The very people who are shocked by reading detailed accounts of prison life would never question the basic concept of justice that has created and maintains the prison system itself. I am not trying here to justify the *bagne*—far from it—but I am trying to point out that one cannot censure the abuses of the *bagne* without broadening that censure to include the basic issue. Our penal institutions are the logical result of our concept of justice by punishment; in creating the prison, society does not so much protect as revenge itself upon the criminal. How ridiculous to pretend that that revenge should be humane! In every sadistic prison act, in every blow struck by a brutal guard, in every hour a man spends rotting in a dark, barren cell, there is the tacit participation and consent of an entire society. If this basic truth is not faced by the authors and readers of such books as

René Belbenoit's *Dry Guillotine*, then the only excuse for writing and reading such exaggerated and sensationalized accounts of life in the *bagne* is that they appeal to the morbid in all of us and make lots of money for their authors.

We prisoners did not speculate philosophically on our lot. Our one dream, our one constant preoccupation was escape, but otherwise we accepted the routines of prison life and did the best we could to get along with them. We tried always to stay on the good side of the guards and this wasn't always easy. The guards, in fact, were often more brutal and more corrupt than the criminals they supervised. They were recruited mostly from the dregs of society, many of them from Corsica; they had little or no education, and they were entirely unequipped for their responsibilities. This isn't surprising. What prison has guards who are college graduates and humanitarians? There are no saints behind bars and very few outside them. We stayed as clear as possible of the worst of these men and managed to get along all right with the others.

During the early 1930s in St. Laurent, there were about 400 men who worked, like myself, in jobs that left us a good deal of freedom. These men were mostly trained workers in various fields—bricklayers, masons, carpenters, artisans of one kind or another. An equal number of men worked the land, either as gardeners for civilian administrators or on their own separately maintained plots, where they grew much of the colony's crop of fruit and vegetables. And there were perhaps a thousand men on permanent fatigue duty. They kept the roads clean, trimmed lawns and hedges, painted the houses monthly, loaded and unloaded boats and trucks, did all sorts of odd jobs. The agriculturals and unskilled workers did not enjoy quite as much freedom as myself and the chosen 400, but their daily life was

far from unbearable. At night, of course, we were all locked
into the camp barracks, but in every barracks there was an
active social life. The men read, talked, wrote, and gambled.
It was not much different from and not much worse than army
life.

This was the way it was in the main camp of St. Laurent.
The same conditions, needless to say, did not exist in the other
camps—at Kourou, in the jungle around St. Jean, on the islands, in Cayenne itself. Life varied from camp to camp, depending partly on the sort of work the men were expected to
do, partly on why they were expected to do it (whether they
were being disciplined or being given routine job assignments), partly on what sort of man was in charge of the camp.
In an isolated camp administered by a sadistic commandant,
men could and did suffer and die. At St. Jean, for instance, a
bad commandant could kill off hundreds of men a year and
two or three did so. Even under the best administration, St.
Jean was no picnic. The work was hard and the climate horrible, stifling and humid. There were insects and poisonous
snakes and vampire bats to contend with. If the men were not
adequately fed and cared for, they succumbed quickly. When
one reads in the popular press of the horrors of life on Devil's
Island, one is usually reading an account of life in the camps
of St. Jean. It was at St. Jean that the worst crimes were committed and men suffered the most. But St. Jean was only one
and not the largest of the penal colonies in Guiana. Most of
us in the *bagne* never experienced the extreme suffering un-
dergone by the minority at St. Jean during that colony's worst
periods.

It wasn't too long before my own life in St. Laurent became
quite pleasant. My skills were much in demand, since I was

the only artist in residence at that time. In addition to such regular mundane duties as painting signs, I supervised the décor at official, semi-official, and purely social functions. I counseled administrative wives on color schemes and painted portraits of their children. I found time to do a lot of outside work for civilians, who paid me quite well for my services. By prison standards, I soon became quite rich; I could afford liquor and cigarettes and all the extra clothing I needed. And, sewn into the pages of my books, I stored away money against my next escape. My freedom to come and go as I pleased during daytime hours became almost absolute and, after a year or so, I was allowed to move out of the barracks and into a small private bungalow close to one of the camp gates.

I made no close friendships during these early years in the *bagne*. Close friendships with other men have never been my forte and I was never tempted to indulge in the homosexual practices that were rife in the camp. Friendship, after all, is much like love, in the sense that there is a partner who loves and one who allows himself to be loved, but it offers few of the real compensations of love. Also, all of us in the *bagne* were terribly concerned with ourselves, our own fates and fortunes, our own likes and dislikes. Too much was at stake for any of us to be truly unselfish, truly loving with one another. Because I was so much better off than most of the other men, especially after I had acquired living quarters of my own, it was dangerous for me to take anyone too deeply into my confidence. Nevertheless, I had no enemies among my fellow convicts. Everyone knew me, I never refused anyone anything— money, cigarettes, wine, clothing—and I was trusted. However, I kept my distance, I bided my time, and the months passed into years.

By early 1934 I was again making plans to escape. I had several thousand francs hidden away, more than enough to acquire a good boat and the necessary provisions for a long trip. I planned to recruit three other men for the venture and set sail for the Caribbean, the surest route to freedom. I had not yet matured these plans when I made a serious mistake.

Need I confess, in view of my earlier history, that my blunder had to do with a woman? Well, it's true. Maria, Paulette, and Marilyn had not taught me to be sufficiently prudent. I embarked on a love affair with a half-breed Indian girl.

Since moving into my bungalow, I had been able to resume my relationships with women. Naturally, I had come to a financial understanding with the guards at my camp gate. The ladies came early in the evening and left in the early morning and the guards always managed to be looking in some other direction at the time. It was an ideal arrangement, provided I watched my step, made sure everyone's palm was caressed, and didn't make the mistake of falling in love with an hysterical or talkative woman.

My half-breed was, of course, hysterical and talkative. She strolled past the gate at night, singing and cracking raw jokes. The guards told me to warn her. I did so and it made no impression. By then it was too late for me, because I had become fond of her and was unable to break off the relationship. I was even blind to the fact that she was simultaneously carrying on with a high official of the camp.

The day finally came when I was summoned to camp headquarters. I knew that something serious was up because two guards came to fetch me. They brought me straight to Colonel Frank and remained in the room during the interview.

The colonel was not pleased to see me. "Stand at attention

Boredom and discomfort awaited us inside the punishment cells.

when you speak to me, Lagrange," he snapped, in reply to my greeting. "And wipe that smirk off your face."

I stiffened and waited. Colonel Frank did not waste time with me. "So you still haven't learned anything from your years with us, Lagrange? You still think you can escape?"

"No, sir."

The colonel's eyes bulged dangerously. "No? No?" he said, his voice rising alarmingly. "Do you mean to say you haven't been plotting all this time to acquire a boat and say good-by to us again? You mean you're going to deny that?"

I said nothing.

"I warn you, Lagrange," the colonel continued, wagging a finger under my nose. "You tell me the truth or you'll pay dearly for lying to me! Now, one more time, Lagrange. Are you or are you not preparing to escape?"

"Every man in the camp is preparing to escape, Colonel," I said. "I'm no different from anyone else."

The colonel slammed his hand down on the desk. "Is that so, you impudent bastard! Then I'll teach you and every man in this camp, if necessary, what the price is! A little tour on the islands might give you some idea! You know what they say about the islands, Lagrange?"

"No, sir."

The colonel smiled unpleasantly. "That you always know the date of your arrival there," he said, "but never the date of your departure. You can think that one over for a while. Take this prisoner out of here!"

The guards seized me by the arms, led me away, and locked me into a solitary-confinement cell, buckling my feet to the iron bar at the foot of the cot.

"My God, Lagrange," one of the guards said to me before leaving, "you're crazy!"

*Feeding the animals condemned to solitary
confinement on St. Joseph.*

"But what did I do?"

"You mean you didn't even know you were bedding down with the colonel's girl friend? Lagrange, you're too dumb to live!"

15 Tourism, Third Class

ALTHOUGH, by all the rules, I should have gone up before the Special Maritime Tribunal and stood trial for my alleged escape plot, Colonel Frank was powerful enough to circumvent the official procedures. After two days in my uncomfortable cell, I was put on board one of the administration launches and taken directly to Royale, where I was officially transferred to the penal colony of the *Îles du Salut*. I passed another horrible night in an even more uncomfortable cell and, in the morning, I was brought to the office of the commandant of the islands, a Corsican named Luccioni.

The interview was swift and to the point. Luccioni, a heavyset, glowering man with black eyebrows and thick, untamed hair, looked me up and down, spat out the window of his office, and cleared his throat. "You look like an educated man," he said. "Can you read and write?"

I blinked with surprise; the commandant evidently hadn't even bothered to glance at my dossier. "Yes, sir," I said.

"Good," Luccioni said. "You'll work here. We need a clerk. Don't make any stupid moves and you'll get along all right. Otherwise you'll wind up on St. Joseph, like the two men before you. Understand?"

"Yes, sir."

"Now get out," Luccioni said, scratching himself. "The sight of you bores me."

That first full year I spent on Royale gave me a real taste of the horrors of prison life. Luccioni, Julien Bonnard's predecessor, was a brutal and corrupt official whose character and methods were faithfully reflected in the treatment the men received at the hands of his guards, especially the Corsicans. The only prisoners who fared well under his regime were those who also happened to be Corsican; they could do no wrong and could get away with just about anything. The rest of us, the vast majority, got along as well as we could, but it was a bad period for the men on the islands and especially bad on St. Joseph, where the guards had everything their own way and could do with the wretched *incos* almost anything they wished. I watched my step; it was a year in which to avoid mistakes. I kept to myself, went about my tasks, never complained, and waited for something to turn up. Something eventually did.

Early in my second year on Royale I was summoned to the commandant's office and presented to a young, pleasant-looking naval lieutenant named Aires. A French cruiser had anchored that morning off Royale and I guessed that Lieutenant Aires was a member of the crew. It turned out, however, that he was not one of the ship's regular officers but in charge of an entirely separate mission. I liked the looks of him. He had an open, smiling countenance and his eyes were intelligent and friendly.

Luccioni opened the conversation with his customary graciousness. "That's him," he said, indicating me as if I were something too loathsome to name. "Ask him. If he can't do it, Aires, no one can."

"*Monsieur* Lagrange," Aires said politely, "I'm anxious to

find out whether you can be of any help to me. My name is Aires and I'm in charge of a hydrographic mission attached to the cruiser you probably saw in the bay this morning. Do you know anything about hydrography?"

"No," I answered truthfully, "but I know something about topography. I could learn."

"Good," Aires said. "We're a bit shorthanded for the job and we could use another man. We've been entrusted with mapping the entire coast of Guiana and the principal rivers, bringing old navigational maps up to date and creating new ones wherever necessary. In going through the files at St. Laurent I came across your name and, from your background, it occurred to me you might be just the man we need. I've already secured permission from the commandant of St. Laurent to attach you temporarily to our group. You'll live on board the ship and be directly under my orders during the term of the mission. Of course," he added with a smile, "I don't want to force you to come with us if you don't wish to. Commandant Luccioni informs me you've been most useful to him here."

"I'd be very glad to come, sir."

Lieutenant Aires turned to the scowling Luccioni. "I hope it's all right with you, sir?"

Luccioni grunted in his most ingratiating manner. "Take the bastard," he said.

For the next few months I worked and lived on board the cruiser as we mapped the coastal waters of Guiana. Though most of the men on board the ship looked askance at me during the first few weeks, Lieutenant Aires treated me with the same respect and courtesy he used toward every member of the crew and, because of his example, I was eventually accepted as a bona fide member of the expedition. I was given civilian clothes to wear and no one ever referred to my convict status or to the unpleasant reality that, once the mission was done, I would have to be sent back to Royale. There were days when I even forgot myself that I was a convict and that I would soon be reclaimed among the ranks of the *bagnards*.

After we had finished mapping the coastal waters and several of the smaller rivers, we steamed up the Maroni for St. Laurent, where we would be stationed for several weeks during the charting of that majestic stream. Before the ship docked, Lieutenant Aires called me into his cabin. He told me what a splendid job I had done for him all these months and wanted me to know that he was most grateful for my help. He added that he was looking forward to my continued collaboration in St. Laurent. "We'll have a good deal of time ashore, Lagrange, and I'm sure that will be welcome for all of us," he said.

"Yes, sir, it will."

Lieutenant Aires looked at me shrewdly. "You also know that after this job, Lagrange, I'll have to send you back to Royale."

"Yes, sir."

"It would be perfectly natural if, during our time in St. Laurent, you were to try to escape," Aires continued. "I wouldn't blame you myself."

"That's very understanding of you, sir."

"Unfortunately, Lagrange, it would interfere with the success of the mission."

"Yes, sir."

"So I want you to give me your word of honor, Lagrange, that you will not try to escape as long as you're under my jurisdiction."

I smiled. "The word of honor of a convict, Lieutenant?" I said.

"No, not as a convict, Lagrange," Aires said. "Your word of honor as one man to another."

Well, he had me there. I could hardly betray this decent man and I didn't want to, but Lieutenant Aires had certainly anticipated my line of thought. Rather than return to Royale and the regime of Luccioni, I had decided most definitely to make another attempt to leave the *bagne*. My only chance was to try it while we were in St. Laurent and now Aires had made that impossible.

Filled with gloom, I nodded. "You have my word, Lieutenant."

Aires stood up and shook my hand. "Good, that's all I wanted to hear from you, Lagrange." I turned to go. "And don't look so gloomy," the lieutenant continued. "We've been assigned to St. Laurent for a period of three weeks, but I expect we'll finish the job in two. That last week I intend to give the members of the mission a leave. You may be interested to know, Lagrange, that I myself plan to spend a few days in Paramaribo. Though still attached to the expedition, you will not be under my direct jurisdiction during that time. Do I make myself clear?"

I turned back to face him. A look of absolute understanding passed between us. I shook his hand warmly, thanked him, and went out on deck to watch our arrival in St. Laurent.

During the next two weeks I continued my work for the hydrographic mission, but I had enough time ashore to plot and organize my second escape attempt. Because I was dressed in civilian clothes, I had no trouble getting about and my purchases in the various stores of St. Laurent aroused no suspicion (I had managed to secrete successfully nearly half the money I had made previously in St. Laurent). Of course I was recognized by many of my former fellow convicts, but word of my

special assignment had gotten about and no one thought anything of my wanderings in the streets of the town, even when
I appeared to be loaded down with suspiciously large amounts
of equipment—canned goods, dried foods, cigarettes, alcohol,
clothing, tools. From a Chinese merchant, the only man in St.
Laurent who probably understood what I was up to, I acquired
a very good secondhand compass, a .22 rifle, and a shotgun. I
stored these supplies in the back room of a small shack I had
rented on the outskirts of town and I waited for the end of the
mission and the departure of Lieutenant Aires.

However, I was not planning to go it alone this time. My
first day back in St. Laurent I had gone to the camp and run
into Leblanc, the old pickpocket who had shared my cell during the early days of imprisonment. We had begun to chat
and it had soon become evident that Leblanc had lost all of his
former enthusiasm for life in French Guiana. Though the
climate had indeed cured his rheumatism, Leblanc longed to
return to the carefree life of the city streets and the exercise
of his profession. "It's not so bad here," he grumbled, "but my
God, Flag, it's boring. I cut grass all day. I'd do anything to
stop cutting grass." I took him into my confidence, told him
of my own plans to escape, and asked him to recruit a third
member for the attempt, preferably someone young and strong.
"I know just the man," Leblanc said enthusiastically. "Powerful as a bull and too dumb to figure out anything for himself.
He'll do just what we tell him. His name is Hercule, they use
him to lift the big weights down at the dock. He got drunk and
strangled his wife one night, but he's a very nice fellow, docile
as a lamb. And he doesn't talk much."

I told Leblanc that Hercule, who was evidently aptly
named, sounded just right. Leblanc was in his sixties, I've
never been physically overwhelming, and we needed a man

who could do a lot of heavy work clearing our way through the bush. I had decided that the inland route offered us our only chance. I knew nothing about navigation or how to manage a small boat, either in the swift currents of the Maroni or on the open sea, and I couldn't trust the two or three men in the camp who did. Our one chance, admittedly a long one, was to make a wide inland detour through Surinam, far enough away from the towns to avoid the risk of being caught by the bands of Indians and bush Negroes who functioned, especially along the river banks, as professional manhunters, getting so much a head for each captured fugitive. I hoped eventually to make the border of British Guiana, where I felt sure we could arrange passage for the Caribbean islands.

Today, looking back on this project of mine, I can't imagine what made me think I would succeed. No one, to the best of my knowledge, has ever escaped through the bush and made it either to Brazil or to British Guiana. Furthermore, I had had the living example in Paramaribo of the fate of those who do attempt the bush. How I could have persisted in my plan in the face of all the evidence is a mystery. I must have been made truly desperate by the renewed prospect of a return to Royale and Luccioni. It was certainly the single most foolhardy venture of my entire career, in prison or out, but attempt it I did.

On the day of Lieutenant Aires' departure, I sent word to Leblanc and Hercule that we would leave that very night. My timing turned out to be fortunate, because, strolling down the street in late afternoon, I came face to face with Colonel Frank. I had not seen him since my arrival in St. Laurent and, from the expression of incredulity on his features, I realized with some misgivings that he had not been informed of my temporary assignment. I decided to treat the encounter lightly.

"Good afternoon, my colonel," I said, stepping respectfully aside to let him pass.

The colonel froze, his mouth opening and shutting, his eyes bulging with unbelief. "Lagrange!" he said at last, gazing wildly around for possible help. "Lagrange, what is the meaning of this?"

"I'm sorry to upset you, sir," I said. "It wasn't my idea, really. I was the only man available."

"Available? Available for what?" the colonel asked, still keeping an eye out for a potential rescuer.

"They didn't tell you, sir?"

"Tell me what, you villain? That you escaped? But we'll soon fix that! I'll see you——"

"Colonel, I'm on a temporary assignment here."

"In civilian clothes?" the colonel shouted. "Oh, no, Lagrange, you don't fool me with such childish inventions! Don't move or I'll have you shot down like a beast!"

Smiling apologetically, I produced my papers and handed them to him. Warily, Colonel Frank took them from me and glanced through them. When he had digested the contents, his dismay changed to fury; the blood mounted up his neck and turned his face into a glowing red bulb. "We'll see about this, Lagrange," he said, fixing me with a malign stare. "I'll take this right to the commandant!"

"It was the commandant who suggested me, sir."

"Damn you, Lagrange, when I want your observations, I'll ask for them!" the colonel said. "After I tell him the circumstances, he'll see it my way, all right!"

"I didn't know she was your girl, sir."

The colonel stepped up to me. "Lagrange, I'll have you back on Royale by tomorrow night, you see if I don't! Now step aside, *salaud!*" And Colonel Frank strode rapidly past me and around the corner.

After this unpleasant encounter, there was no longer any possible question of delaying our escape. Colonel Frank would most certainly carry out his threat, the commandant would investigate, it would be discovered that Lieutenant Aires had left and that the expedition had finished its work, and I would immediately be shipped back to the islands. I was not prepared to allow Colonel Frank such an easy triumph.

That evening, shortly before mess time, Leblanc, Hercule, and I met at a prearranged spot on the outskirts of town, waited until dark, then struck out along the route I had carefully calculated some days before. If we marched all night we could count, I had estimated, on about twelve hours before anyone would miss us. The barracks' guards had been bribed—a usual procedure in all such escapes—and, with normal luck, no alarm would be given until after the morning roll call. By that time we expected to be twenty to twenty-five miles away, in the process of making a wide loop around St. Jean. The first search parties would hunt for us along the river banks, but we would avoid the river until well beyond St. Jean, crossing it far upstream at a narrow, fordable spot near an abandoned gold mine, about thirty miles north of the *relégué* camps. After that, we would strike inland again, skirt the Dutch settlements, then cross the border into British Guiana, connect up with the Essequibo River, and follow it down as far as Georgetown, on the coast. From Georgetown we would find some way of getting to the Caribbean.

The plan made sense on paper, as most plans do, but it could not possibly work out. No one who has never attempted to travel through the South American bush can imagine what it's like. One has to hack one's way foot by foot through the

jungle, climb mountains, cross swamps and streams, under constant, savage attack from the insect life, in killing heat and
humidity. I am ignoring such added hazards as the bushmaster,
the coral snake, the fer-de-lance, the copperhead, the water
moccasin, the anaconda, the vampire bat, the peccary, the
jaguar, and the alligator because, with luck, you can avoid
them. The basic conditions of life in the bush no one can avoid;
only people used to those conditions can survive even for short
periods. Needless to say, we were not used to them and we
suffered horribly.

By morning we had covered approximately twenty miles, at
a tremendous price in physical discomfort and desire. As we
sat around our fire, trying to shield our swollen faces and hands
from the rapacious mosquitoes, Leblanc urged turning back.
Hercule was undecided. He had done the bulk of the work,
but, thanks to his tender twenty-four years, he was in better
shape than either Leblanc or myself. For my part, I was still
absolutely determined to go on; I couldn't believe that the situation wouldn't improve and I had my vision of Colonel
Frank's apoplectic face to spur me on. I brandished the shotgun at Leblanc. "I'll kill the first one of you who turns back,"
I said, bluffing royally.

Leblanc groaned, but Hercule managed a smile. "He's right,"
he said to our waverer. "It would be sad to quit after one day."

"That's the spirit," I said eagerly. "In two days we'll be on
the river again and we can rest there for a while. It can't be
this bad on the Surinam side."

Leblanc looked at me hopelessly. "Why can't it?" he asked.

"It just can't," I insisted idiotically. "Anyway, we'll get used
to it after a while."

"You're crazy," Leblanc said and hid his head under a blan-
ket to escape the insects.

I will not dwell in detail on the appalling miseries that beset us during the next two days. Miraculously, we did somehow manage to cover about forty miles, making our detour around St. Jean and coming back at last to the river bank. We just did survive. In fact, if I hadn't pushed on by myself and come within sight of the river, we would have made camp in the bush that night and perhaps died there. Leblanc was at the very end of his rope, Hercule was running a high fever, and most of our supplies had had to be discarded en route. It had become no longer a question of escaping, but one of mere survival.

We spent the next two days recuperating beside the river. Our situation was still serious, since our supplies were running out, but, as our physical condition improved, our morale rose and we again talked of escaping. That is, Hercule and I talked of it; Leblanc was all for returning to St. Laurent. Finally, we decided to compromise. We would build a raft and try to cross the Maroni to the Dutch side, where we could try our luck with the Dutch authorities in the inland villages and, hopefully, continue on to British Guiana. If we failed to get across the river, we'd proceed downstream and give ourselves up.

The new plan made about as much sense as the old one. We knew very little about building rafts and nothing at all about the river itself. The Maroni looks placid enough, but its currents are deceptively strong and tricky, and a sudden squall, not at all uncommon on the river even in the dry season, can convert it into a dangerous torrent. We were to learn all this the hard way.

No sooner had we launched our absurd craft, made of logs lashed clumsily together with vines, and started to pole out into midstream than the current swept us away from the shore and propelled us rapidly along. The raft spun wildly about, forcing us to drop our poles and hang on. Then, after twenty minutes of this, we were drenched by a tropical downpour and the river started immediately to rise. The raft, spinning faster and faster in its headlong descent, now began to come apart. Hercule and I jumped into the water and clutched its more solid-looking timbers, but Leblanc refused to stir. Having obviously abandoned all hope, he sat rigidly in the middle of the collapsing raft, waist-deep in water, and waited for the end. "By God, Lagrange," he said through clenched teeth, "my whole life spent on the streets of Paris and I die like a drowned rat in the middle of a jungle! If we ever meet in hell, I'll even things up!"

Leblanc had been too pessimistic; we were not destined to meet in hell quite yet. Not one of us could recall later exactly what happened. The next thing I myself remember is waking up on the bottom of a large pirogue, being paddled along swiftly by six husky, naked Indians. We landed beside a tiny native village on the French side of the Maroni and there I was soon joined by my companions, who arrived in separate canoes. Leblanc's memory was even hazier than mine, but Hercule did recall crashing into something and the Indians told us later that they had picked us up, more dead than alive, on the beach of a small island. Anyway, we were happy enough to have survived at all. Our saviors gave us some bread and *tafia*, and, as soon as we could walk, we were taken into the village and presented to its leading citizen, a plump, amiable-looking man in his forties, who smiled, nodded, and indicated that we should sit down opposite him.

Hercule and I did so, but Leblanc hung back. It was evidently his first contact with Indians, and who knows what fears were racing through that small street-urchin mind of his.

I turned to him and addressed him in talkie-talkie, the universal pidgin language of the river, so as not to offend our host. "Come, man, don't be fraidie," I said. "We talkie-talkie on——"

"You may speak your own language, *Monsieur*," the Indian said in perfect French. "I understand it quite well."

I was astonished, since I had never heard of an Indian who spoke such flawless French, and I gaped at the man. He laughed and introduced himself to us as Captain Pita, head man of this small village belonging to the Galibi tribe, and he went on to inform us that he also spoke excellent English, Spanish, and Portuguese, all of which he had picked up as a young man during his wanderings about South America. "Unlike most of the members of my tribe," he said, "I have always been curious about the outside world. Now that I am past my youth, I am content in my own village. That's life, is it not? Now, how may I be of use to you gentlemen?"

Leblanc and Hercule announced that they wished to return at once to St. Laurent. They had had more than enough of the fugitive life and they felt that, if they gave themselves up of their own accord, they would be treated leniently by the prison authorities. Captain Pita said that he would put a canoe and a crew at their disposal that very afternoon; then he turned to me. "And you, *Monsieur*?"

I shrugged fatalistically. "It won't go so well with me," I said. "I was due to go back to Royale anyway. This time they might send me to St. Joseph."

Captain Pita nodded sympathetically. "Then stay here with us for a few days," he said. "We can decide later what to do."

"I'm sorry, Flag," Hercule said, putting one of his huge hands on my shoulder. "We can't get out through the bush and I'd be lost in Surinam. I don't speak Dutch or German, they'd catch me right away. But you, you'd make out all right."

Leblanc snorted contemptuously. "Sure," he said, "he'll make out all right. We'll see him back in the *bagne* in no time. What a fool I was to listen to him!"

"No hard feelings, Flag?" Hercule said, a worried frown on his heavy, stupid, kind face.

I shook his hand warmly. "No hard feelings," I answered. "Good luck."

A few hours later, Leblanc and Hercule left for St. Laurent. I remained in the village as the personal guest of Captain Pita, who turned out to be an extraordinary man, self-educated, intelligent, considerate, and loving. He was adored by everyone and his word was law. During the week I spent in his hut he was a regal host and we spent entire evenings talking on every conceivable subject. In fact, we were fascinated by each other. He told me stories of his wanderings through South America, especially of his experiences as a sailor and later as a captain on board various small coastal sailing ships, and I enchanted him with tales of my adventurous life in the world of crime. I also endeared myself to his villagers by helping them with the elaborate tattooing of their bodies, a practice much in vogue among the Galibi. At the end of my sixth or seventh day in the village, Captain Pita offered me permanent citizenship in the tribe. "Dress and mark yourself like us," he said, "and they'll never catch you. Two or three more weeks in the jungle and you won't even look like a white man. Also, the men from the prison rarely come up this far. When they do, we could easily hide you."

"I'm very touched by your offer," I said, "but I'm afraid I don't really belong here. Besides, even if my friends keep quiet, word is sure to get back eventually to St. Laurent that there's an escaped convict living with you. I'll only get you into trouble. No, Captain, I'll have to leave you and the sooner the better."

Captain Pita thought it over for a few seconds, then quietly agreed with me. "You're right, of course, it would never work," he said. There was another silence, then he looked up at me again. "How would you like to get to British Guiana without having to go through Surinam?"

"I can't think of anything I'd like more."

"Do you have enough money to get along there?"

"Yes, for a while."

"You'll need new clothes. We can buy some for you on the way."

"The way to where?"

Captain Pita then explained that he and his three oldest sons were planning to leave in a couple of days to go turtle hunting along the Guiana coasts. The best hunting grounds for the huge sea turtles, which are considered a delicacy by the Indians, are near the mouths of the larger rivers, on whose beaches the turtles come to spawn. In their large sailing canoe it would be no hardship, Captain Pita assured me, to go as far as the Berbice River in southern British Guiana. There they would put me ashore and I could presumably make my way to Georgetown by myself. I accepted this generous proposal with gratitude.

Three days later, seated comfortably on the bottom of Captain Pita's roomy pirogue, I once again sailed past St. Laurent. The trip was not without its anxious moment. Almost directly opposite the town the wind died and for ten or fifteen minutes (it seemed a full hour to me) we floated lazily along at the whim of the current, which was taking us uncomfortably close to the shore. Captain Pita, who was at the helm, began to summon the wind in the traditional Indian manner, by whistling. However, his selection was not an old Indian melody, some plaintive chant calculated to bore the god into compliance, but a bouncy, accurate rendition of "Lolita, Flower of Java," a popular song of the day. Instead of being offended, the god responded enthusiastically; the sail filled and we quickly left St. Laurent behind.

For the next two weeks we sailed slowly up the coast of Surinam, hunting and fishing as we went. By the time we reached British Guiana and the mouth of the Berbice, the pirogue was full of bloody egret feathers, drying fish, and turtle blubber. Though I was sorry to say good-by to my good friend Captain Pita, I can't say that I was heartbroken to leave his vessel. We landed on a flat, sandy beach, Captain Pita and I toasted each other in *tafia*, I donned the white suit and tennis sneakers he had bought for me in a small Dutch coastal village, we all embraced one another, and I was left to my own resources.

It seems strange to me now that I didn't understand at once how the British authorities learned of my presence as fast as they did. I had been careful to keep my suit clean and pressed during the trip (I had stowed it in a box under the prow of the boat), I had shaved and trimmed my hair, and I was confident that I looked as respectable as any other citizen. But when, an hour or so later, I boarded a bus bound for Georgetown along the main coastal road, odd things began to happen.

The bus driver made no difficulty about accepting francs instead of the local currency, but when I leaned over to hand him the money he shot me a startled look and turned his head away. I walked to the rear of the bus and sat down. A couple directly in front of me got up and moved forward. Their action triggered a mass exodus from the seats around me. Within a few minutes I found myself alone, the other passengers

bunched up toward the front of the vehicle. I was so happy
to be back in civilization that I didn't immediately notice the
curious behavior of the bus's occupants, but by the time we
reached the outskirts of Georgetown I realized that something
was seriously wrong. Not only were the other passengers avoiding me but they conferred together from time to time and
turned periodically to stare at me. Rattled, I got off at the next
stop.

Everywhere I went in Georgetown that afternoon the experience repeated itself. People ignored me until I was within
a few feet of them, when they would suddenly glance suspiciously around, spot me, and withdraw in horror. To escape
this alarming attention, I fled into the comforting darkness of
a movie theater. Half the audience rose en masse and stam-
peded for the exits. I followed them out and took refuge in a
public park, where at last I seemed to be safe. There were few
people about and I was able to sit down and attempt to un-
ravel the mystery. Carefully, I went over my whole outfit, but
I could find nothing wrong with it. Had my years in prison so
changed my appearance that anyone could now spot me for a
dangerous escaped criminal? It didn't seem possible; yet what
other explanation could there be for the odd behavior of
Georgetown's citizens when confronted with my presence? I
could find no answer. I played it safe and remained in the park
until well after dark.

Late that evening I wandered into a slum section of the
town and booked myself a room in a seedy waterfront hotel.
Even here the clerk looked at me askance and backed away
from me. In the solitude of my room I undressed and waited
sleeplessly for the morning. Sure enough, at about 5 A.M.,
there was a knock on my door. When I opened it, I was confronted by a tall, immaculate policeman in a khaki uniform.

"I'm afraid I'll have to ask you to come along with me," he said, gazing at me with profound distaste.

I resigned myself to the inevitable. "All right, one minute, if you please. I'll get dressed."

"I'll wait in the hall," the policeman said, backing away from me.

"One moment," I said. "How did you spot me? Do I look like a convict?"

"I don't know what you are, my good fellow," the policeman said, "but I do wish you'd take a bath. You can't come into court stinking like that. I don't know what's the matter with you vagrants; you look decent enough, some of you, but you ought to be forcibly disinfected. Hurry up now, I haven't got all morning, you know."

So there it was. During my weeks among the Indians I had grown used to their odor and it had become a part of me. Blended with the fragrance of dead fish and turtle blubber, it must have enveloped me in a cloud of near-poisonous gas. In fact, it must have taken me days to get rid of it entirely, since no one during my entire stay in Georgetown ever lingered in my presence long enough to finish a conversation with me.

Though I was arrested for vagrancy, I had given myself away to the policeman and in court my real story quickly came to light. I was told by the judge that it was not the policy of the British authorities to extradite fugitives from the *bagne*, but I was told I was an undesirable alien and given eight days to leave British Guiana. There was nothing I could do about it and I didn't have enough money to book passage to any of the Caribbean islands. I took the only course left open to me and fled into Venezuela.

It was only delaying the inevitable. The Venezuelan authorities were no more pleased to see me than the British ones.

I was arrested, released, rearrested, re-released—a pattern that persisted for weeks. Finally, I was given twenty-four hours to leave and told that if I didn't I would be put to work on a road gang. I knew what that meant, at least several years of forced labor for the government of dictator Gómez, with no hope of reprieve and the eventual prospect of death from malnutrition or disease. I could see no difference between the *bagne* and a Venezuelan road gang, so I fled again, this time to the Dutch island of Curaçao.

I survived in Curaçao for over a month by managing to stay out of sight, but eventually I came to the attention of the local Dutch authorities who, with characteristic Germanic efficiency, looked into my background and at once contacted the French penal administration. Three weeks later I was back in St. Laurent, waiting to go up before the Special Maritime Tribunal. This time I knew I could expect a formal sentencing and a swift return to the *Îles du Salut*.

Colonel Frank was delighted to see me. "Well, *Monsieur le touriste*," he said, "tired of your vacation? How was it in the Bahamas? Or did you spend most of your time in Miami? We've missed you. Oh, yes. However, you'll be so busy from now on, you may never want to leave us again."

16 The Islands

*T*ʜᴇ sun rises in a blue sky over the *Îles du Salut*. The sea in the early morning is usually calm, even during the winter months, and it breaks endlessly against the black rocks of the island shores. The palms rustle softly in the breeze. The bell that strikes at dawn to awaken the sleeping men is the one that strikes at dusk, recalling us to our cells, our barracks, our rooms. The sound of that bell marks the passing of the day; it punctuates our routines, we live by its tolling. In the early mornings we are summoned by it to our tasks, moving in the cool half-light in groups of fifteen or twenty or thirty to the duties of the day. Some of the men work on the roads, on the buildings, in maintaining the grounds; others harvest the coconuts used to feed the pigs and chickens that provide much of the meat we eat; others report to the houses where they are employed as handy men and servants; a few of us, the literary types, take our places in the administrative offices, at desks piled high with papers. The men are forbidden to talk on their way to and from work, so that only the voices of the guards are heard as they bark out the orders everyone already knows by heart. From within the hospital, the church, the bakery, the cell blocks where men lie in darkness and count the seconds, the mysterious sounds of prison life begin to fill the air. Another day, no different from any other. A space in time, indistinguishable from past and future. A monotony, a waiting, a gray infinity of purposeless seconds. The sun rising and setting, the bell tolling, the guards shouting, the small tasks and evasions and the rare, fleeting pleasures snatched from a day, any day, summer, winter, fall, spring, season after season. This is prison life, the life of the islands, the life I was to know for the next five years, from 1937 to 1942.

It wasn't easy for me at first because I chose to make it difficult for myself. After my return to St. Laurent and my sentencing by the Special Maritime Tribunal, I gave up hope. Both my escape attempts had been failures, I knew what my life on Royale would be like under Luccioni, and my sense of humor deserted me. I was sullen and talked back to the guards. The result was that I was immediately placed in solitary confinement on Royale, with nothing to do all day but lie on my hard cot in a dark and tiny cell, my only contact with the outside world at mealtimes, when we were fed through small openings in the steel doors that barred us even from prison society.

Oddly enough, this dismal isolation from the world of men turned out to be my salvation. Cut off day after day from the petty preoccupations of camp life, I was suddenly overwhelmed by a desire to paint again. Not the sort of painting I had been doing for Colonel Frank and others—flattering portraits of their wives and children, idealized sketches of themselves, facile illustrations of their home life—but the sort of work I knew I could do, the sort of work I had to do. I wanted to paint the *bagne*, to record and interpret for myself as well as for others the life of the penal colony as I had seen and known it.

Luckily for me, one of the guards assigned to my cell block was extremely corruptible. For the few francs I was able to pay him, he smuggled in canvas, paint brushes, and small cans of house paints, and with these crude supplies I set to work on the series of paintings that I was to complete years later, after my release from prison, and that are today in the private collection of Mr. Bailey K. Howard, the president of Field Enterprises Educational Corporation in Chicago. Work on these paintings kept me from going mad during the weeks I spent in Cell 16 of my barracks on Royale, not only by keeping me occupied hour after hour but also by restoring a sense of purpose to my life. I was never to lose it again.

While I was in solitary, Luccioni's regime came to an end and I was released from my punishment cell. Under his successor, Julien Bonnard, life on the islands became more bearable for the men in general and much more enjoyable for me. I decorated my church, I continued to work on my paintings, and the days passed, no longer empty of meaning. After Bonnard had gone back to France and been replaced by another commandant of the Luccioni stripe, the situation deteriorated once more, but I never again lost hope or the desire to stay alive and do my own work, no matter how bad things became.

I don't wish to perpetuate here the impression given by every other book and reportage I've ever read on the *bagne*, and especially on the islands, that everything was terrible all of the time. As I've said before, in considering the *bagne* and prison life in general, one has to bear in mind the concept that created and preserves the system of punishment by imprisonment. It is inevitable that this system lead to suffering and abuse. However, apart from individual acts of injustice, life on the islands was no worse in many respects and better in some than life in the other camps. The greatest hardships were endured by the *incos* on St. Joseph. For most of us on the islands, life was routine, subject to many of the same rules and disciplines we had become accustomed to on the mainland.

On Royale things were rarely very bad. If we did our jobs and obeyed orders, we were not abused. With the few francs we could earn doing odd jobs around the island we were even allowed to buy a few luxuries—foodstuffs, tobacco, wine. During our leisure hours in the barracks we could talk or read or gamble. Two or three of the men could play the guitar or the mandolin and some of the evenings were passed listening to music. Life in the barracks could be and often was convivial, so convivial that most of us preferred to live in the main dormitories rather than occupy the few available individual cells. These cells were most often reserved for the prison outcasts, men who for one reason or another were detested and shunned by their fellows. A few men lived in them by choice, merely because they favored solitude, but the other occupants were the perverts, the bullies, the informers, the lunatics of the camp.

On St. Joseph, of course, it was different. Men sentenced to months and years of solitary confinement enjoyed no privileges. They couldn't smoke or buy food and wine or enjoy one another's company. If they were being punished for some infraction of the rules, they were allowed out of their cells only half an hour each day, to walk in silence around an enclosed courtyard under the cold, watchful eyes of their guards. The rest of the time they lay on the wooden boards of their cots, their legs fettered to an iron bar, or huddled miserably on the stone floor of their cells, staring up at the shaft of light coming from one small aperture in the ceiling, waiting, waiting, if only for the next meal. If they were not being punished, they were allowed out each day to work. They were set to hammer-

ing at the countless rocks of St. Joseph, to carrying these rocks
from one place to another all over the island, from the shore to
the highest point and back again, hour after hour, day after
day of meaningless, brutalizing labor. This was the lot of the
incos, most of whom were serving sentences ranging from five
to ten years for persistent refusal to abide by the rules of the
bagne.

The politicals on Devil's Island, the men who had been
found guilty of treason, lived a physically easy life. They were
not compelled to work and they were better fed than the rest
of us. Of course, their isolation was permanent and complete,
and they must have suffered a great deal from it. I remember
seeing one of them pacing every day along the coast, walking
swiftly, blindly back and forth, back and forth like a caged
animal. I wouldn't have traded places with that wretched man
for anything in the world.

Whatever our individual lot on the islands, we prisoners all
had one thing in common: we lived under the constant scrutiny and often at the mercy of our guards. And yet, oddly
enough, it was not a simple question of oppressors and op-
pressed, of masters and slaves. The guards were men like ourselves, in their way as much the victims of the prison system
as we were. Their lives, their hopes and desires were inextri-
cably entwined in ours. They depended upon us as much as
we depended upon them. There was a saying in the *bagne*
to the effect that we were all—convicts, guards, and functionaries—prisoners: "In the *bagne,* one half watches the other
half." We were all dressed in the uniforms of the system, the
guards in severe white, the prisoners in red and white stripes,
but, after a while, one ceased to make even such visual distinctions. One became merely a man among other men, a victim among victims. The distinctions became individual, not

based on status but on the common denominator of humanity.

Contrary to what has been written on the *bagne*, the guards were not all assassins. They had the power to punish, but it was a power they usually exercised reluctantly. They were as lazy and as anxious to short-cut the inconveniences of the system as we were; they, too, adopted the colonial pace. There were atrocities, veritable crimes, but they were not committed by the guards merely because they were guards, but by individuals, by men because they were men, subject therefore to the madnesses that afflict all of us. The guards were no better and no worse than the men they guarded. They had become guards because, for most of them, it was a relatively easy way to earn a living. They came from the lower classes of society, from the slums of the cities and the barren fields of Corsica, and that, too, they had in common with the majority of those they guarded. Their one desire was to get through the working day with a minimum of inconvenience and to snatch from their daily routines the few pleasures life afforded. They made the compromises and adjustments that are made by everyone everywhere. They justified their selfish actions by hypocrisies; they secreted their bestialities under a cloak of professed virtue; they blustered and bullied in order to hide their cowardice and self-contempt. They were men.

The crimes of the *bagne* cannot be blamed on a particular group of people, the legion of trained, uniformed sadists imagined by the popular press, but rather on the individual and on the society that empowered that individual to act. We were all as guilty as we were innocent, as helpless to do away with the *bagne* and the guillotine as we were instrumental in creating them. This was the reality of the *bagne*, the reality that all of us consciously and unconsciously lived with for the years of our terms, guards and convicts alike. I blame no one and I blame everyone. If, later on, I speak of specific crimes, of specific acts of cruelty, it is not because I wish to feed the human hunger for horror, but only because I wish to speak of what I know, of what I feel, of what all of us endured. The punishment does not justify the crime, but neither does the crime justify the punishment. If the *bagne* I knew no longer exists, it most certainly exists elsewhere. The injustices and atrocities I write about are being duplicated at this very moment in prisons everywhere. It is important to understand this, because a prison is a prison, whether it is located in St. Laurent or in Paris, on Devil's Island or on Alcatraz.

In writing about the *bagne*, you see, it is easy to make general accusations and to make them stick. Where all are equally guilty and equally innocent, the finger can point in any direction and find a culprit. For instance, I accuse the government of having created and maintained the penal colonies in French Guiana. I accuse society of having created the government. I accuse mankind of having created society. More specifically, I accuse the guards of having served as guards. I accuse the *bagnards* of being *bagnards*. I accuse the islands of being islands, the jungle of being jungle, the climate of being a climate. In short, I accuse the world of being what it is.

It was on the *Îles du Salut* that I became fully aware of having participated from the very beginning in the universal conspiracy. If I go on now to write of the smaller crimes I have witnessed and participated in and heard about, it is because I can do so out of this awareness that we are all guilty of the one big crime of being born.

17 Crimes and Criminals

STEALING was certainly the most common of all the crimes that were committed in the *bagne*, though it was not, of course, the only one. The thefts were mostly petty ones and for the purpose of making life a little bit more comfortable. That is, as far as the convicts and the guards were concerned. We stole food, clothing, tobacco, wine, and money, from one another and from the administration. But the biggest robberies and swindles were perpetrated by the officials who occupied the more privileged positions. After all, the loftier the height, the lower one has to stoop.

Colonel Frank, for instance, had organized a little smuggling ring. His trusted convicts were placed in key positions inside the prison commissary system, and the goods flowed endlessly across the Maroni and into the markets of Surinam. He was never caught, but one of his successors was. To avoid the scandal and having to face trial, this bold fellow appeared in the streets of the town one day dressed only in his shirt and dragging a great cluster of pots and pans along behind him. He ran around shouting that the end of the world had come and evidently it made a strong impression on everyone. He was relieved of his duties and sent quietly back to France to recuperate. He was never brought to trial.

Then there was the case of the high official in Cayenne who dabbled in real estate. To clear the land and build the houses he sold to civilians and other high officials, he made liberal use of convict labor. This cut down his overhead and soon made him a rich man. He got into difficulties only when it was discovered that the manpower and equipment he was using should have been employed in the construction of a new prison. He was officially reprimanded.

There was the commandant of the islands who summoned me to his office one morning and made me a curious proposition. "Lagrange," he said, "I want you to make me some American money. I want to play a joke on a friend of mine." I told him that I would need a press, the inks, above all, the paper. The commandant had all these things. How many dollars did he need in order to play his joke? "Oh, five or six hundred will do," he said nonchalantly. I made him $600 and he promptly asked for 600 more. It must have been quite an elaborate joke, but I never found out on whom he was playing it. "You understand, Lagrange," he said to me with a smile, "this will remain between us, eh?" He left on leave a week later and never came back. An odd rumor went the rounds on Royale to the effect that the commandant had quit the service and gone to America. Perhaps the man he was playing the joke on lived in the U.S.A.

Not all the administration thieves went entirely unpunished. Some of them were actually relieved of their duties, one or two of them became *bagnards* themselves. Others were troubled by their consciences. One of *Monsieur* Bonnard's successors was so dismayed to hear that serious objections were about to be raised to his embezzlement of administration funds (the convicts had been complaining for months about the absence of meat from the prison menus and the large reduction in the clothing allowance) that he took the trouble to hang himself. He was buried with honors on St. Joseph, in a touching ceremony that left all of us dry-eyed with emotion. It was generally agreed that he had taken an unrealistic view of his position, since his superiors would certainly not have hung him for his crime.

The administration was curiously reluctant to chastise too severely the dedicated men who toiled in its behalf, though it was quick enough to mete out justice to the *bagnards*. Perhaps this was because it did not wish to upset the social order of prison life. After all, if one admits that the crimes of one man are indistinguishable from the crimes of another, regardless of his uniform or social position, then the entire premise upon which the prison system rests becomes almost untenable. Stronger minds than those of mere penal officials reel at the thought. No, a prisoner is one kind of man; an official in the exercise of his noble calling is another.

For example, consider the case of the two guards who, strolling along the banks of the Maroni one night, witnessed the escape of a group of prisoners in a small boat. Quickly, they commandeered a pirogue and set off in pursuit of the fugitives. Unfortunately, they were too late to catch them on the opposite shore. Rather than admit defeat, they paddled down to a nearby Indian village to make inquiries. They found that the men of the tribe were away and that the women claimed they knew nothing about any escaped convicts. The guards decided to question one of the younger women more closely. They took her to the beach. One question led to another. The young lady unreasonably refused to remove her clothes. The guards were sure she was concealing a weapon, so they stripped her. The young woman made what the guards took to be provocative gestures, so they raped her. After all, men are men, *Monsieur le juge*. Upon their return, the guards filed a full report of the incident and were commended for their diligence. The Indian woman, evidently an accomplice, had been lucky to escape with her life. That was the judgment handed down by the penal court of inquiry in St. Laurent. Actually, it should never have gone that far at all, but the shameless Indians had had the temerity to protest and some official action had to be taken. The court was apologetic about it.

Murder, of course, could be awkward. There always had to be some sort of investigation and a lot of time was wasted. It was a relatively simple matter if it was merely a case of one convict eliminating another one. The convicts always killed one another, usually with knives, for the same reasons. They quarreled over money, over gambling rules, over lovers. Ultimately, it never mattered what the reasons were. The guillotine on Royale settled all the accounts, answered all the questions. The culprit was tried and sentenced to die. Early one morning he was taken from his cell, given the last rites by the island priest, made to lie face down under the blade, and separated from his life. That evening his corpse would be rowed out to sea by his fellow *bagnards* and dumped unceremoniously into the water. This was the standard form of burial for convicts on the islands. The body, like that of his victim, would never reach the bottom because the sharks, ever present and long-accustomed to the taste of human flesh, were always waiting. They made a clean, quick, savage ending of every dead *bagnard*.

Occasionally, a convict murdered an official, in which case the investigation might be a little more complicated (for one thing, the official's family had to be informed of the circumstances in some detail), but the verdict never varied. The blade

There was an active social life inside the barracks.

of the guillotine always fell, a head always rolled, the sharks were always fed. Sometimes, however, the murderer was an official and then the situation could become deplorably sticky. The investigation had to be taken seriously and the killer could not always be acquitted. He was never forced to submit to the guillotine, of course, but his career was sometimes jeopardized.

During my first year in St. Laurent, a guard named Antona killed a man and was actually brought to trial for it. He had been overseeing a road gang a mile or two outside the town and had repeatedly warned his charges not to wander out of sight. One of the men had ignored his warning and had headed for the bushes. Antona had shot him through the neck.

That was his version of the story and it probably would have been accepted without question by the court, despite the contradictory testimony of the other convicts (the testimony of a convict is not taken very seriously in a French court), if the event had not been witnessed by a certain *Madame* d'Imbert, a civilian lady who had been sunning herself on the nearby terrace of her house at the time. She informed the court that Antona had refused to allow the men to rest or even to relieve themselves. Finally, one of them had headed for the bushes. Antona had shouted to him to stop. The man had answered, "Listen, I've got to go and do what even you can't do for me!" Antona had waited for the man to turn around and had then shot him.

The court accepted *Madame* d'Imbert's version of the killing and Antona was severely punished. He was lowered one grade in rank and transferred to another prison.

The most hated and feared man on the islands during the years I was on Royale was a Corsican guard named Filidori. Fortunately, he was assigned permanently to duty on St. Joseph, where he was in charge of one of the punishment cell

The sharks around the islands were always well-fed and became accustomed to human flesh.

blocks, and I never had anything directly to do with him, though I saw him from time to time whenever he chanced to be visiting Royale. He was a heavy, muscular, hairy man of about fifty, with the face of a professional thug. He had already killed two men in the mainland camps and had successfully pleaded self-defense each time. In addition to his regulation pistol, he wore a knife in his belt for "the heart to heart," as he called it. He claimed that one could never be sure of a pistol and that the knife was a necessity. He had killed his second man by carving him to death. A killer, a bully, a torturer, he was detested by the *bagnards* and shunned even by his fellow Corsicans.

There was a wretched convict on St. Joseph at that time named Berthé, who had been sentenced to solitary confinement for repeatedly trying to escape. He was harmless enough, but he had become a nuisance to the guards. He was always whining and complaining and writing long letters to the administration about the mistreatment he had been receiving at the hands of one functionary or another. All the prisoners, even the *incos,* had the right to complain in writing and some of them abused the privilege. Berthé was one of these. He made the serious mistake of saying in one of his letters that Filidori was the scourge of the camp.

One night the door of Berthé's cell opened and Filidori walked in. He unfettered Berthé's ankles and ordered him to stand up. Berthé fell to his knees and pleaded with him. Filidori closed the door of the cell and drew his pistol. "To the wall!" he said. Berthé resigned himself to the inevitable. He crawled to the corner of his six-by-nine-foot room, turned his back, and waited for death. He did not wait more than a few seconds. Filidori shot him in the back. The bullet tore through Berthé's chest and embedded itself in the wall.

Filidori tore a few buttons off his shirt, scratched his face, and again pleaded self-defense. He claimed that Berthé had lured him into his cell on the pretext of being ill and had attacked him. The guards were not supposed to enter the cells of the prisoners after dark without special permission from the officer in charge, but Filidori, motivated by humanitarian considerations, had considered it his duty to answer the plea of a suffering man. When Berthé had attempted to strangle him, he had had no choice but to shoot him.

No one believed this story, but the administration was quite prepared to accept it. The fact that Berthé was a weakling and a coward, certainly not the sort of man a brute like Filidori would have had any trouble handling, did not seem to preoccupy anyone. We all expected Filidori to be acquitted and returned to his duties.

Unfortunately for him, the doctor involved in the case, a young man new to the ways of the *bagne*, performed an autopsy on the victim. His findings contradicted Filidori's account of the events. Berthé, the doctor revealed, had been shot in the back and the bullet had passed out through his chest, opening a rather large hole in it. Furthermore, he had been shot from a distance of three or four feet. The scratches on Filidori's face and neck, the doctor maintained, could not have been made by Berthé's nails, as Filidori claimed, because Berthé had no nails to speak of; he had bitten them all away.

The doctor's testimony embarrassed everyone. Filidori was asked to turn in his pistol, though not his knife, and he was discharged from the service. The severity of the punishment caused some muttering within the offices of the penal administration and the doctor was treated with evident contempt by a few of the older hands. As for us, we didn't care whether Filidori was punished or not, but we were glad to see him go.

Some months later we heard on Royale that justice, ever poetic in its workings, did finally catch up with Filidori. One of the men he had killed on the mainland was a fellow Corsican named Santoni, a bravo with hordes of male relatives. They had not forgotten him and they had not forgotten the name of his murderer. When Filidori left the *bagne* and arrived in Marseilles, a large welcoming committee had gathered to greet him. His body, full of interesting stab wounds, was discovered two days later in a back alley of the Marseilles waterfront.

The fate that eventually caught up with Filidori did not prevent other men from following in his footsteps. Occasionally, the murders were executed with Machiavellian skill. There was a guard on Royale who hated one of the convicts because he suspected the man of having had relations with his wife. The convict worked as a houseboy in the guard's bungalow and the wife was undoubtedly a lady of questionable virtue. The rumor was that she had been a prostitute in France and had come to Guiana to escape her profession. She had met and married her husband in Cayenne and she had been putting horns on him ever since. We all knew that she had slept with most of the other guards on the island, so why not a convict? In any case, the husband became suspicious and laid a trap.

Every morning, during the time he knew the *bagnard* would be working in the yard, either feeding the chickens or cleaning the area or hanging up the laundry, he made his wife go outside and stretch out provocatively in a deck chair. She was to let the convict see as much of her as he could and to be very nice to him.

The wife must have understood what her husband was up to, but she was frightened and she did as she was told. She was experienced and she was very good at her tease. The *bag-*

nard was serving a life sentence, he had no homosexual inclinations, and he could not, of course, resist the view morning after morning. When he finally cracked and ventured to reach for the promised merchandise, the husband was prepared. He had been waiting, day after day, behind the closed shutters of his bedroom window. As the *bagnard* made his move, the husband had only to open the shutter and shoot him down.

As far as the court of inquiry was concerned, it was a simple case. The husband had returned home unexpectedly to find that his wife was being brutally attacked. He had done what any husband would have done. The court agreed. He was acclaimed for his virtue and his wife became less free with her favors. The luckless *bagnard* kept his rendezvous with the sharks.

My favorite criminal during all the years I spent in the *bagne* was a Corsican guard named Giorgi. He was a plump, good-natured, rosy-cheeked man in his forties who had a high-pitched, ready laugh and sported a heavy mustache. Of the Corsicans it was said that they grew up to be either guards or convicts and this saying was doubly true of Giorgi, who had spent most of his life in prison in one capacity or the other. He was an absolute realist about the penal system, considering it nothing more than a farce whose sole object was universal injustice. Giorgi was perfectly willing to participate in the farce and pay it lip service as long as he himself was able to exploit his role to his own advantage. He had a finger in every racket in the camp and there wasn't a convict under his command who didn't at one time or another help him steal. In prison, stealing comes as naturally as breathing and we were all delighted to pitch in and give Giorgi a hand because he was very popular. He always paid off his accomplices generously and he never allowed institutional discipline to interfere with his mission in life, which was to enrich himself at the expense of the state. He never punished the men for anything and no one, therefore, ever betrayed his confidence or abused the freedom he dispensed so lavishly.

As far as I know, he was never caught for any of his thefts, which seems miraculous to me now because some of them were really stupendous and so many people were involved in them. Boatloads of supplies vanished mysteriously up the Maroni; entire warehouses in Cayenne were stripped bare; caravans of convicts tramped through the bush making his deliveries and pickups. During his service on Royale I myself participated in several raids on the commissary and I was never rewarded with less than a bottle or two of *tafia* or a five-pound sack of coffee or a tin of tobacco. Giorgi always kept his word, paid on time, and protected his men.

He made a real fortune as a gold smuggler during the years when gold was still at a premium on the international market. He was too smart to try running it out through the bush or hiding it among other merchandise. He knew that the customs officials were extremely severe about gold, though they were inclined to overlook other items. Giorgi melted his ore into forks, spoons, knives, small plates and ash trays, *objets d'art*, souvenirs of Guiana. The gold flowed out in people's pockets, in their hand luggage, always openly. The customs officials never weighed anything and Giorgi was soon able to buy himself an estate and retire to his native island, where, for all I know, he is still living in luxury. We were all sorry to see him go. My last memory of him was of a summer day during the war, shortly after the fall of France. I was then back in St. Laurent and we were all, guards and prisoners, summoned to a rally in the main square of the camp where the new commandant asked us to shout allegiance to Pétain. The hurrahs were faint indeed, but one voice, high-pitched and clear, soared out above the others. "Hurrah for money!" it shouted. It was our friend Giorgi, declaring openly his true allegiance.

I have spoken in this chapter specifically of the crimes committed by guards and officials of the penal administration. Why? Because the *bagnards* were not criminals? No, because we were *all* criminals, we *all* committed crimes. The guards and officials lived in the *bagne*, they abided by its morality, they were *bagnards* like ourselves. That is to say, they were not, with rare exceptions, concerned with justice or such abstract questions as the abuses of power. They were men who wanted to get along, keep quiet, get away with what they could, and save a little money. I have recorded here only the crimes I have seen and known about during my own term in the *bagne*.

18 *And So We Leave Beautiful Royale....*

Most of the men serving time on the islands had been sent there originally for attempting, like myself, to escape. No one was supposed to be able to escape from the *Îles du Salut*. The islands lie ten miles directly offshore and are surrounded by open, shark-infested sea. The prisoners worked during the day under the constant supervision of the guards and at night they were locked into their barracks or chained to the cots of their cells. How was it possible for any-one ever to escape? It wasn't possible, but many tried and a few actually succeeded.

The more desperate and impractical fugitives built them-selves crude rafts, usually with improvised sails, and counted on the wind and current to take them to the mainland. If they were not caught right away, they almost all perished. The sea overturned their craft, feeding them to the sharks, or swept them directly into the mouth of the Sinnamary River, where the confluence of the sea and river currents creates whirlpools and a sucking surf in which even the best swimmers are likely to drown. If, miraculously, they did make the shore, they died in the swamps or in the bush. The ones who were recaptured right away were lucky.

Amazingly enough, repeated failure discouraged no one and some attempts were truly ingenious. A Russian I knew discovered that coconut shells are extraordinarily buoyant. He made himself a huge canvas sack, dragged it down to the tip of the island one night, stuffed it full of shells he had been storing away in a hole for weeks, and launched himself into the current. By dawn he was at the mouth of the Sinnamary, where he hung on to his raft through the pounding of the surf, and he was eventually washed up on the beach. Fortunately for him, he was too battered and exhausted to risk the bush and he was recaptured that very afternoon.

If the guards had been incorruptible, of course, it would certainly have been impossible to escape or even to attempt it. The only time to try was at night and no one could leave his barracks or his cell without the consent or the complicity of one or more guards. This was also largely true of the mainland camps, but it was absolutely true of the islands. The penal administration was never betrayed by nature—the bush, the swamps, the sea, the climate, the sharks, the mosquitoes, the snakes, all were faithful, honest servants. Only the beings who were paid to serve could be and were always corrupted.

Probably the most brazen escape from the islands was the one organized by the men whose job it was to unload supplies at the pier on Royale. They were all Corsicans and they had no difficulty in arriving at a price with their guards, who also happened to be Corsican. Not for them the crude escape by raft. They left one evening in the administration motor launch and docked the next morning at Georgetown. The French had no extradition agreement with the British, who, for their part, did not consider escape from the Guiana penal colonies a crime at all. It looked as if the Corsicans would get away, but a clever French official pointed out to the British customs authorities that the prisoners were planning to sail on into the Caribbean in a boat belonging to the French Government. The British reacted with alacrity. Stealing a boat was definitely a crime—piracy, in fact—and should not go unpunished. The Corsicans were immediately apprehended and turned over to the French authorities. They were all sent to St. Joseph, where they were eventually joined by two of the guards who had collaborated with them. The price for that collaboration had been 75,000 francs, too large a sum for even the administration to overlook. How the Corsicans had managed to lay their hands on such a huge amount of money remains a mystery.

The most elaborate and clever escape ever made from Royale (no one, as far as I know, ever got away from either Devil's Island or St. Joseph) took place only a few months after my arrival there. It was brilliantly conceived and executed by the men who worked in the camp bakery and it became famous throughout the *bagne* as "the escape of the bakers."

The bakery that supplied bread for all three of the islands was located near the little harbor of Royale, not more than a couple of hundred yards from the pier itself. It was a large, square, whitewashed structure and it contained three huge ovens that were eight or nine feet tall and stretched the full width of the building. There was a space of three or four feet between the tops of the ovens and the ceiling.

Twelve men were permanently assigned to work in the bakery, four of them at a time in shifts of eight hours each, and they toiled under the supervision of three guards, one to a shift. The bakers were among the most trusted prisoners in the colony and the guards were never overly vigilant; besides, it was too hot in the bakery for a man dressed in a full uniform and a pith helmet and carrying a heavy gun. The convicts worked and sweated inside, the guards remained outside.

Among the more recent recruits in the bakery was a clever young Pole named Czerny. He very soon made some interesting discoveries. First, he found out that two of the ovens could easily take care of the daily needs of the camp. Secondly, he learned that the guards never entered the building at all and that one of them was easily corruptible. Finally, by cautiously sounding out his fellow workers, he ascertained that seven of them were quite as eager as he to escape should the opportunity ever present itself. Czerny set about creating that opportunity.

The corruptible guard was corrupted and a watch was posted on the other two; one of the men was told to give an appropriate signal every time the guard on duty happened to stray too near the door. Through the good offices of their bought official, it was relatively easy for Czerny to arrange that the four recalcitrant bakers would work one of the day shifts. Though they were not planning to participate in any escape attempt, they could be trusted to keep quiet. They could also be trusted not to use one of the ovens. When all of these preliminary arrangements had been completed, Czerny put his plan into action.

The top of one of the ovens was removed and the bricks were stored under some flour sacks in a corner of the building. One man stood guard, two men baked bread, the fourth climbed into the empty oven and set to work building a boat. The metal for the frame was supplied by the camp blacksmith, another Pole and a great friend of Czerny's. Other sources of supply yielded canvas, paints, rope, and boxes full of prison overalls. The overalls, made out of a tough, water-resistant cloth, were torn into strips and used to lash the frame of the

boat together. It was hot, slow, tedious work, but in six weeks
Czerny and his bakers built inside that roofless oven a sailing
canoe thirty-three feet long and about six feet wide. It was
fully provisioned and solid enough to withstand anything but
the most severe storm.

Late one night, during the shift of the corrupted guard (at
the inquiry, he successfully pleaded sudden illness as the reason for his absence from his post), the bakers slid their boat
out of the oven, loaded it with provisions, raised the mast, un-
furled their sail, ran with it down to the water, climbed in,
and set off for the continent.

They got as far as Paramaribo. Knowing about the Dutch,
Czerny had wanted to continue beyond Surinam, but several
of the men were too seasick to go on. The Dutch took them
into custody and thoughtfully contacted the French authorities. The bakers were all brought back to Royale and transferred to St. Joseph. Except for Czerny. In Paramaribo, he
succeeded in bringing his case to the attention of the Polish
consul, who secured his freedom and repatriated him. We
were all delighted to hear of his success. As for the canoe itself,
it was put on exhibit and can still be seen today in the small
museum of Paramaribo. It testifies to the fact that when a man
really wants to arrive at something, his ingenuity will overcome all obstacles.

My favorite escape was most certainly the one attempted
by a friend of mine named Seznec. He was an amusing man,
slight, bald, excitable, full of droll stories and wild jokes, but
it was hard to believe in anything he said. He was entirely
obsessed with the idea of escaping and he was convinced that
he alone would succeed. "Why does everyone else fail? Why,
Flag?" he would say to me. "Tell me that! Why?"

"Because it's very difficult," I always answered.

Seznec would slam his hands together and bound about. "No!" he would shout. "No! It's because no one ever tries to make it alone, that's why! Aren't I right?"

"No," I would say, "you're not right. Many have tried it alone, but they always get caught or killed."

Seznec would stop bounding about and lean close to me, his shrewd little eyes glittering triumphantly. "Ah, not *really* alone, Flag!" he would say. "There's always a brute of a dumb guard in the picture! No matter what you pay them, they always talk. No! You watch the way I do it! You wait and see!"

This conversation, or some variation of it, was liable to occur several times a day and it was impossible to take Seznec seriously. We all thought he was an amiable crackpot who enjoyed hearing himself talk and that he liked to make himself feel very important and daring. I certainly never dreamed he would actually try to put his theory into practice or I would have done my best to dissuade him.

Seznec had several jobs on Royale and he enjoyed a certain amount of freedom. He tended the cemetery behind the church, fed the priest's chickens, did odd tasks around the hospital, and harvested coconuts. In his wanderings around the island he would stop from time to time, between errands, to snatch a quick smoke in a small privy that had been erected behind the church. It was while he was sitting in the dark privacy of this refuge one day that he had his great vision. "Flag, I'm going to do it!" I remember him saying to me. "I've found the way!"

I thought nothing more about it. Seznec was always full of great ideas, projects that couldn't fail, schemes that were absolutely foolproof. I didn't notice that our familiar daily ritual conversation concerning the proper method of escape no longer took place or that Seznec suddenly began to keep much more to himself. He seemed to be animated by some great secret enthusiasm, but I was too wrapped up in my church murals at that time to pay much attention to him.

Late one afternoon, having finished my work, I came out of the church to have a cigarette before returning to my barracks and I saw a strange sight. Seznec staggered past, the privy strapped to his back. "Seznec!" I said. "What are you up to?" The little man looked up at me fiercely. "Shut up!" he hissed. "I'm moving the privy. What does it look like I'm doing? Remember, you haven't seen me!" And he lurched off down the hill.

That night we heard that Seznec had been caught trying to escape. For weeks he had been smuggling pitch, glue, canvas, nails, and other supplies into the privy and he had been working bit by bit to transform it into a boat. Several of the guards had seen him moving it down to the shore that afternoon, but he had told them that Father Perrier had instructed him to take the object down to the sea and give it a good scrubbing. He had worked over it until dark, right under the eyes of the whole island, then had set it afloat, climbed in, and waited for the current to sweep him to freedom. Unfortunately, he had been spotted right away by a guard who happened to be strolling with someone else's wife down by the shore and the administration launch had quickly towed him back into harbor.

Seznec's escape attempt became the joke of the island, but I found out later how close he had come. He had done a first-rate job of calking and waterproofing, and, to give his unique craft added buoyancy, he had strapped empty kerosene cans to its sides. When a few of the guards, to amuse themselves, tested the privy's seaworthiness a few days later, they discovered to their astonishment that Seznec's peculiar craft could support nearly a ton.

Poor Seznec! No one complimented him on his achievement and he was sent to languish in a cell on St. Joseph. But if it hadn't been for the adulterous dalliance of a guard, he might have succeeded in achieving the most sensational of all the many escapes ever made from the *bagne*.

As for me, I was never tempted to try my hand at escaping from Royale. I had made two rather noble attempts from St. Laurent and they had both ended in failure. On the islands, the odds against success seemed very long and I knew that another failure would mean incarceration on St. Joseph. I had had my taste of solitary and I was not anxious to sample it a second time.

More important, I had my own work to do. In addition to my regular duties around the camp, I continued to paint, first in the church and then for myself. It had become the main concern of my life and the only real sustenance I had against the wearying monotony of prison life. The days succeeded each other endlessly, one exactly like the other, and it was this sameness, this routine passing of time that wore on everyone, guards and convicts alike. None of us knew when, if ever, we would leave the islands. We existed in a blank, a limbo, cut off, perhaps forever, from contact with the outside. The more imaginative and sensitive a man was, the more difficult it was to bear this isolation. If it hadn't been for my painting, I'm sure I would have cracked under it and certainly wound up on St. Joseph.

World War II broke out in Europe, but it made no difference to us on the islands. Life went on very much as before, even after the fall of France and the creation of the Pétain government. We did hear rumors of a mass prison break from the mainland camps, but they were only rumors and we did not take them seriously. Among the officials, a few old faces disappeared and a few new ones took their place, but that was all. There was no change in policy or in the way the *bagne* was administered, at least not at first. I began to think that only the end of the world would ever free me from Royale.

Then, in July 1942, I was called into the office of the new commandant, a stern-looking old soldier who had recently publicly declared in Cayenne that he considered Marshal Pétain the savior of his country and had been rewarded for his zeal with command of the islands. To my amazement, the old warrior stood up when I walked into his office and shook me by the hand. "Lagrange," he said, "you've been reprieved. My felicitations!"

After a few seconds, I was able to stammer out a question. "May—may I inquire, sir, how—how this—this came about?"

The commandant informed me that Marshal Pétain had declared a general amnesty for all convicted war veterans and that my splendid record during World War I had been brought to the attention of the penal authorities. "My friend," the commandant said, again squeezing my hand, "our country is great and merciful and it calls to everyone of us in its hour of need. I know that you, as an old soldier like myself, will not let her down."

I am ashamed to say that I was too astounded to honor the commandant with the appropriately flowery reply I am sure he expected.

19 *March or Die!*

*T*HE reprieve was conditional. It did not mean that I was a free man, but it did mean that I could leave the islands and return to St. Laurent, where I would be allowed to reside outside the camp. I would not have to wear the convict uniform, but I would still be subject to the prison regulations and continue to work for the penal administration. I was told that if I kept my nose clean and stayed out of trouble I would become a full-fledged *libéré* within two or three years. "You're a lucky man, Lagrange," one of the guards told me on the day I left Royale. "You're the only *bagnard* to be reprieved this year. See that you don't come back here."

"Don't worry," I told him. "Nothing is ever going to bring me back to the *Îles du Salut!*"

As soon as I landed in St. Laurent, I reported at once to the director of the camp, my old friend Colonel Frank. Naturally, I was nervous, but I soon discovered that the colonel had apparently mellowed a good deal over the past five years. In fact, he received me if not with warmth at least with a somewhat detached and preoccupied air. "Oh, Lagrange," he said, "yes, we've been expecting you. Have you been assigned living quarters?"

"Not yet, sir."

"Well, well, all in good time," the colonel said. "I suppose you'll want to live outside the camp?"

"Yes, sir."

"Well, why not, why not?" the colonel said, passing a hand wearily over his eyes. "Go and get settled, then. Report here in the morning."

"Yes, sir. Thank you, sir. Will I be working for you, sir?"

The colonel shrugged hopelessly. "My God, how should I know?" he said. "Everything's a mess. How do I know what you'll be doing, Lagrange? Or what any of us will be doing two weeks from now?" I stared at him in some surprise, I'm sure, because he suddenly jumped to his feet, the picture of his former self. "Where the hell have you been, Lagrange? Don't they tell you anything on the islands? Don't you know there's a war on? That France has already lost it? That we don't know from one minute to the next what to do or who to listen to? Pétain says one thing, De Gaulle says another, and we don't even know where the money is coming from to keep this place going? And now they're about to send us a new commandant, some old fool from North Africa! Wake up, man! How the hell do I know what you'll be doing? And why should I care? Get out of here! Come back tomorrow! I'll think of something to keep you busy!"

After I had been assigned to a small bungalow not far from the camp itself and moved in, I spent the rest of that first day wandering about the town, reveling in the change of scenery and my first taste of freedom in five years. I soon also became aware of a certain electricity in the air. People stood in the streets and in the bars in small groups, talking together in hushed tones. The discussion was always on the same subject. What was the government up to? Should Guiana follow De

Gaulle or Pétain? Would the Americans invade? What would become of the *bagne* if they did? Why had the old commandant been replaced by Vichy? Was it because he had declared himself for De Gaulle? Was there any truth to the rumor that the new man was a stanch Pétainist? Weren't the Germans winning the war? What if they didn't win the war? But how could they lose? Shouldn't Guiana declare itself neutral? Were the cops and the army for Vichy? What to do, what to do, what to do?!

The next morning I found Colonel Frank more confident and much more optimistic about the future. "Lagrange," he said, "we have work for you, a great deal of work."

"I'm glad to hear that, Colonel."

"I've just received official word that the new commandant will be here in exactly ten days to take up his duties," he said. "Naturally, we all wish to make him feel at home and to welcome him in the most appropriate fashion."

"Naturally."

"Your decorative talents will be required to grace a suitable ceremony."

"Splendid, sir."

"I have it on the highest authority, Lagrange, that the commandant is an ardent patriot, a most loyal follower of the marshal."

"Yes, sir."

"As we all are, Lagrange." The colonel walked to the window and struck a Napoleonic pose, every inch the figure of a conqueror. "There are some who claim that De Gaulle represents the true spirit of France, but they are misguided. In fact, they flirt with treason, Lagrange. Pétain is France! De Gaulle is communism!"

"I see, sir."

The colonel fixed me with his most impressive recruiting-poster stare. "Lagrange, we must all do our duty to the regime," he said. "We must make the commandant aware of our sentiments."

"Yes, sir."

"I have made inquiries, Lagrange," he continued, "and I have been told that there is a grave and immediate need to fill. Despite the long-standing enthusiasm of all of us in French Guiana for the marshal, there are distressingly few portraits of him to be had anywhere. This must be taken care of right away, Lagrange. Do I make myself clear?"

"Yes, sir."

"We will require not only portraits of our beloved leader but also a few representative allegorical pictures symbolizing the glories of his career," the colonel said, carried away by his own eloquence. "Do your duty, Lagrange! As a patriot and an artist!"

Over the next ten days I worked feverishly to justify the touching confidence Colonel Frank had avowed in my ability. I painted twenty-eight portraits of Marshal Pétain and several large pictures depicting triumphant French soldiers sweeping all, or almost all, before them (they did not sweep Germans). Colonel Frank was delighted. He distributed the pictures about the administration offices with orders that they be hung immediately and prominently. "Well done, Lagrange," he said to me, "you are a credit to the Republic!"

The morning before the new commandant was to arrive in St. Laurent, Colonel Frank once more called me into his office. "Shut the door, Lagrange," he said to me. "I wish to discuss a delicate matter." I was surprised, not by the request for secrecy but by the colonel's renewed air of uneasiness. A great deal of the patriotic fervor and breast-beating he had been indulging in for more than a week seemed to have evaporated overnight. I wondered what had happened.

"Lagrange," he said, when I had sealed us in, "American warships were sighted this morning not far from the harbor of Cayenne."

"An invasion, sir?"

"We think not," the colonel said. "Probably just routine maneuvers, you know." He chewed thoughtfully on a nail for a few seconds, then sighed deeply. "However, one can never be sure. It doesn't seem possible that the Americans will ignore us forever, does it?"

"I imagine they regard us with some suspicion, sir."

"Quite so, quite so." The colonel surveyed his chewed nail, appeared to be satisfied with it, and began to nibble elsewhere. I waited patiently for him to finish his meal. "Lagrange," he said at last, "in this world of treachery and sorrow it pays to be prepared." He stood up, removed the large portrait of Marshal Pétain from the wall above his desk, and handed it to me. The paint on the picture was still fresh; I had finished it the day before.

"You don't want the picture, sir?" I asked.

"Of course I want the picture, Lagrange," the colonel said. "It's a splendid representation of our greatest man. However, France is fecund. There are several great men on the scene today." The colonel paused to find the correct phrase. "Lagrange," he said, "I would like you to paint on the other side of this portrait an equally magnificent likeness of France's second-greatest man."

I suddenly saw the light. "Of course you are referring to General De Gaulle?"

"Of course, Lagrange," the colonel answered. "Do you think you can have this picture back for me by tonight?"

"I'll do my best, sir."

"I thought you would, Lagrange," the colonel said. "It is
easier to have one portrait to cover all emergencies than to
have to mess about with several of them. One never knows
when the wrong portrait will pop up. This way we simply turn
the picture over, depending on the circumstance. I am a patriotic citizen of the Republic, Lagrange. I am loyal to the nation, not to any one man. I would not want my patriotism to
be misunderstood."

"Of course not, sir," I said, picking up the picture and heading for the door. "No one could misunderstand your position,
sir."

The double-sided patriotism of Colonel Frank was characteristic of that feverish, troubled period in the life of the
bagne and it cannot be denied that it had its comic-opera aspect. However, the merely amusing part of the situation vanished with the arrival in St. Laurent of the new commandant,
a man who entertained only the highest loyalties to the government of Vichy.

My initial sight of him came on the afternoon of his first
day in St. Laurent. We had all been summoned into the main
square of the camp to hear him make his opening address to
the men, guards, and prisoners alike who would from then on
be under his jurisdiction. It was a customary ritual of the
bagne and no one took it very seriously, though we were all
naturally curious to have a look at our new chief. I remember
being struck at once by the odd appearance of the man. He
was short and pudgy, soft in a rather feminine way, with small,
dainty feet and hands. When he walked, his flesh quivered
underneath his uniform, which, though obviously recently
pressed, seemed wrinkled in peculiar places, as if it had been
expressly designed not to fit him. His face was round, pasty,

smooth, almost unlined, and his thin, short lips were all but completely hidden by a thick Hitlerian mustache. He would have cut a pathetic, rather ludicrous figure if it hadn't been for his eyes, which were very small but magnified enormously by the thick lenses of his rimless eyeglasses. His stare was bleak, expressionless, frighteningly cold.

Colonel Frank, as the ranking officer present, welcomed the new commandant with the usual trite phrases. The two men shook hands, then the commandant stepped forward and, putting his little fists on his girlish hips, surveyed the silent ranks of the *bagnards* for a few seconds. Finally, he cocked his head back and began to scream at us in an extraordinarily high-pitched, nasal tenor. I shall never forget his first words.

"You are all beasts!" he said and paused to let the full effect of this opening sink in. "And because you are beasts and not men," he continued, "you are going to be treated like beasts! You came here to pay for your criminal behavior and, believe me, you are going to pay!" The commandant now began to pace back and forth in front of us, his hands still on hips, while he continued to scream insults at us. "There are those of you who think you will escape from here and join the criminal De Gaulle! You will not escape! If you attempt to escape, you will be sent to the guillotine! France has no need of you! You are expendable! In this prison—and you will learn that it *is* a prison!—you will work to live! I intend to march in a straight line along the course of my duty! You will follow! You will learn to march or die!"

It was an extraordinary speech and we were soon to find out that the little man meant every word of it. The entire atmosphere of the camp changed with his coming; the colonial pace became a race merely to stay alive.

During the next few days I discovered something about this

devilish little man. He had spent most of his career in obscure outposts of France's African colonies, most of the time in and around Djibouti, and had risen by sheer longevity to the rank of colonel. After the fall of France, he had been among the first to declare himself wholeheartedly for Pétain and the Vichy government. He had managed to have himself recalled to the *métropole*, where he had soon become a source of embarrassment to the authorities. Hopelessly incompetent, he was nevertheless so outspoken in his praise of the new order in France that no one dared dismiss him from his post or relegate him to some minor, obscure function. He talked so much about himself and his career in French Somaliland that he soon became known to everybody in his department as Colonel Djibouti, a nickname that was to stick to him permanently. Finally, when it turned out that the commandant of the *bagne* was suspected of being pro-De Gaulle, someone had had the brilliant idea of replacing him with Colonel Djibouti. It was a good way to get him out of France, but it was to cost the rest of us dearly.

Misery now overwhelmed the *bagne*. The rules were strictly adhered to and new, more severe ones were instituted. Brutality became the order of the day. Colonel Djibouti was everywhere, poking his nose into everything, making life miserable for everyone. Men were sent to solitary for the slightest infractions; the guards were given free reign to take any measures they saw fit to enforce discipline; food and clothing allowances were cut to the minimum. The suffering finally became so severe at St. Jean, where the *relégués* were forced to work longer and longer hours in the awful humidity of the jungle, that it led to a mass prison break, the only one I know of in the entire history of the *bagne*.

Nearly half the camp participated in the escape attempt and

several hundred *bagnards* got safely across the Maroni. This time the Dutch authorities refused to co-operate with the penal administration. They considered that the Vichy sentiments of the French in Guiana made them enemies of Holland and they would not extradite fugitives from Axis tyranny. Most of the *bagnards* were allowed to join the Free French and many of them fought in North Africa under De Gaulle, winning their postwar freedom in the process.

Colonel Djibouti went berserk when he heard the news and redoubled his repressive efforts. He personally took command of the camps around St. Jean and instituted procedures that turned out to be disastrous for the men in his care. Every convict was given a daily work quota. If he failed for any reason to fulfill it, his rations were reduced and he was expected not only to do his next day's quota but also the exact amount of work he had failed to do the previous day. If he was unable to make up his full quota, his rations were reduced still further. No excuses were accepted, no allowances at all were made for illness or injury or age. Colonel Djibouti's famous phrase, "March or die!", became an appalling reality. At the time he assumed personal command of St. Jean the colony still contained approximately a thousand men. During the year and a half of his regime, 680 *bagnards* died of starvation, disease, and mistreatment. It was the only period of real mass suffering I ever witnessed in the *bagne* and it was easily as bad as anything René Belbenoit and the other chroniclers of the penal colonies' horrors ever wrote about.

In St. Laurent, after Colonel Djibouti's departure for St. Jean, things weren't quite as bad, but they were bad enough. Colonel Frank managed to have himself transferred to Cayenne and his successor was an ex-guard Colonel Djibouti had hand-picked for his incorruptible sadism. Punishments were frequent, severe, and stringently administered. The men were all put to work on twelve-hour shifts of fatigue duty, and no exceptions were made. The guards were given a free hand and men began to die in St. Laurent as well.

I was lucky; I was not one of the sufferers. My status as a semi-*libéré* protected me from the worst abuses of the regime, and there's no question about the fact that my Pétain-inspired reprieve worked to my advantage. I managed to stay out of harm's way and remain as much in the background of events as possible. Fortunately, along with three or four *libérés*, I was able to give a good deal of help to my fellow convicts. We smuggled food and clothing into the barracks at night and, in a number of other small ways, did what we could to relieve the general suffering. However, it was a losing battle. The men became mainly concerned with staying alive at any cost, since, as in St. Jean, illness was not regarded as a suitable excuse for not working. A sick convict became very soon a dead one. I would estimate that about 200 men died in St. Laurent at this time.

After about eight months of such horror, I was given the chance to get out. One of the high officials of the civil administration in Cayenne was writing a book on Alfred Dreyfus and he needed a man both to illustrate his book and to re-create for him the living conditions Dreyfus had experienced during his years on Devil's Island. He appealed to the penal administration offices in Cayenne and they relayed the request to St. Laurent. The civil official was a big shot in the local government and it would not have been politic for the administration to turn down his request, though I am certain Colonel Djibouti would have been inclined to do so. Naturally, the assignment fell into my lap. I accepted it gratefully and left St. Laurent with no regrets. The daily suffering of the men had become all but unbearable and I preferred the prospect of Devil's Island itself to continuing to live under such conditions.

The book on Dreyfus was never published, which does not surprise me because, from the part of the manuscript I read, it was a very dull work. The author was a career bureaucrat who wrote books as a hobby, the way another man might collect stamps or asphyxiate butterflies. He had high hopes that one of his books would one day be published, but I'm reasonably certain that, if he's still alive, he is still hoping. In any case, the incompetence of his writing did not concern me; I was glad to get the assignment and I left for the *Îles du Salut* with a weird feeling of relief.

For six weeks I lived in one of the small huts on Devil's Island, making sketches and jotting down my impressions from day to day. I was forbidden to communicate in any way with the men actually serving sentences on the island, but otherwise I was allowed absolute freedom. I soon found myself, like the others, pacing the shore line and staring out to sea, listening through the night to the sound of waves washing against the rocks, to the wind blowing through the tops of the palms. As I lay on my cot, hour after hour, I had plenty of time to think about what Dreyfus had endured for five years.

"The hut designated for my use," he had written, "was built of stone and covered about seventeen square yards. The windows were grated. The door was of latticework with simple iron bars. This door led to a little anteroom six feet square, at the other end of which was a solid wooden door. In this anteroom a guard was always on duty. He was relieved every two hours. The guard was not to lose sight of me day and night. Five men were detailed to this duty.

"At night the outer door was locked inside and out, so that every two hours when the guard was changed there was an infernal clatter of keys and iron bars and grates."

Dreyfus had not been allowed to work or even to sit facing the sea, because it was feared that an attempt would be made to rescue him. When a small English newspaper actually published a story to the effect that he had been rescued, additional security measures were taken. A double wall eight feet high was built around the hut, shutting off all view of the outside, and at night Dreyfus was fettered by both ankles to his cot. "When my feet were inserted in the two bands," he wrote, "it was no longer possible for me to move about. I was fastened in an unchangeable position to my bed. The torture was hardly bearable during those tropical nights. Soon also the bands, which were very tight, lacerated my ankles."

His isolation was complete. He existed from day to day like a vegetable, unable to work, to talk to anyone, to look at anything, his every movement watched by another pair of eyes. That he did not go mad is a tribute to the man's character, though it has been recorded that he did occasionally scream into the wind in his anguish. Evidently there were certain tortures not even Colonel Djibouti had been able to improve upon.

During my time on the island I made about a hundred sketches of the place and jotted down several thousand words of impressions. This material was all turned over to the would-be author in Cayenne and I have no idea what became of it. I had even included an exact, detailed map of Dreyfus's living quarters and I'm sure that my work could have been of some real use to a serious-minded biographer. From my civil official I never received a word of acknowledgment or thanks.

When I got back to St. Laurent, things were even worse than they had been. Nor did there seem to be any prospect of an improvement in the situation. One day I saw a guard club a prisoner to the ground in the middle of the town while the rest of us, civilians and *bagnards* alike, stood by and watched helplessly. I made up my mind then and there to attempt another escape, though I knew what the consequences of being caught would be this time.

I had almost completed my plans when everything miraculously changed. I got up one morning and found people running about the streets in wild excitement. The Americans had landed in North Africa, the tide had finally and definitely turned against the Axis. Furthermore, an American naval task force had been sighted steaming toward Cayenne, accompanied by warships of the Brazilian Navy. All over French Guiana the penal and civil officials were hastily re-examining their consciences.

Colonel Djibouti and the more outspoken members of his administration were arrested and locked into a cell block, from where they were eventually sent back to France to share in the pleasures of the German occupation. (I don't know whatever became of Colonel Djibouti, though I'm reasonably confident he must have been tried and condemned for his traitorous collaboration with Vichy. One can only hope that he paid the full price for it.) Mass rallies were held in St. Laurent and Cayenne, at which speakers affirmed their undying loyalty to De Gaulle and the democratic cause. When the Americans landed in Cayenne the next day, they were greeted with flowers and a welcoming committee. French Guiana, it seemed, had always been for De Gaulle. Why had the Allies waited so long before coming to see for themselves?

I was not, of course, in Cayenne on the day of the American landing, but I am certain that my old friend Colonel Frank must have been in the forefront of the patriots. I am even more certain that he remembered to turn his portrait of Marshal Pétain over.

20 *Liquidation*

*I*N 1937, two years before the outbreak of hostilities in Europe, the French Chamber of Deputies had voted to do away with the *bagne*, and from that time no new shipments of convicts had been sent to Guiana. The idea had been to close the penal colonies down gradually, allowing most of the men already there to serve out their sentences, letting the *bagne* fade away bit by bit, one man at a time, camp by camp, until nothing would remain except the memory of it. The process had been expected to take ten, perhaps fifteen years, but the war had interrupted it, then hastened it. Under Vichy, the *bagne* underwent its death agony. After the horrors inflicted upon it by Colonel Djibouti's regime, there was nothing more to do, once peace had come, but to liquidate it. And so, in 1946, the year I received my final reprieve and became again a free man, the authorities organized a Committee of Liquidation to do away once and for all with the penal colonies of French Guiana.

Nothing happened overnight. You cannot do away in a few hours with a bureaucratic organism that has acquired a life of its own and has survived for nearly a hundred years. Then, too, hardly anyone dependent on the *bagne* wanted it to end.

Certainly not the guards and functionaries who profited from
its existence, who led easy lives adapted to the colonial pace,
and who were not above enriching themselves through graft,
petty theft, and swindling at the expense of the state. Certainly not most of the civilian population, which had become
dependent upon it for its livelihood and for the menial, useful
public services only the convicts performed. And certainly not
the *bagnards* themselves, especially those with time still to
serve or under life sentence. What had they to gain? They
would be returned to France to spend their days behind the
grim, gray walls of metropolitan prisons, banned forever from
the sun, from light and air and even the simple joy of being
able occasionally to snatch a smoke, to walk down a city street,
to look up from a labor to see the blue of sky and sea. If the
bagne was not a paradise, it was at least better than the prisons
we had all known at home. The character of man being what
it is, there was no reason to suppose anything had changed.

But the *bagne* had become too notorious to survive. The
whole world knew about Devil's Island and the frightful
abuses of French justice. Better to put an end to it, to allow
the jungle to do its work of obliteration, to close a chapter, and
to silence the ignorant clamor of the outside world. Who would
arise to speak for the men behind the walls in France, or elsewhere, for that matter? What journalist would trouble himself
to write shocking half-truths about the unromantic lives of a
local convict population? The average prison does not lend
itself to romance, not unless it happens to have a name that
captures the popular imagination: Devil's Island! So close the
bagne, tell yourself that the episode is over, let it survive only
in legend, cloak the state in virtue, and allow time and silence
and indifference to do the necessary rest.

The Committee of Liquidation did its work with commend-

> *In the camps around St. Jean the men
> worked like slaves and died by the hundreds
> under the Hitlerian gaze of Colonel Djibouti.*

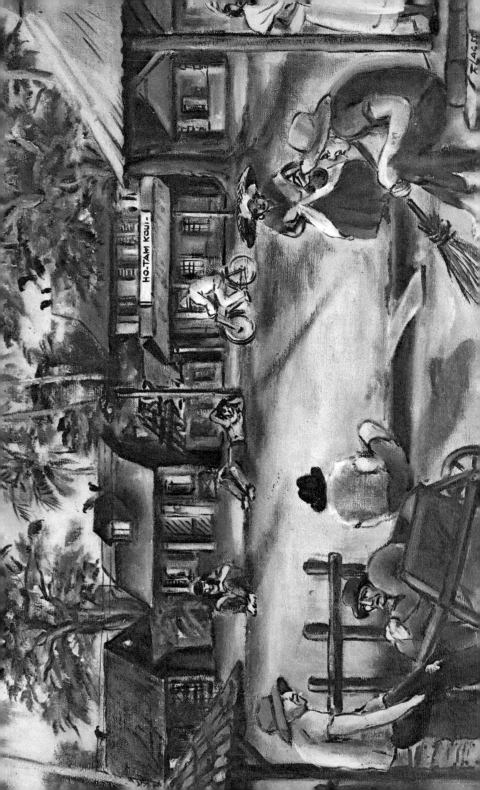

able thoroughness and in a reasonable amount of time. One by one the camps were shut down, the men left, the jungle crept in. The property of the penal administration was disposed of, a great deal of it through dubious channels, some of it on the open market. Certain members of the Committee of Liquidation became extraordinarily wealthy men. "It will be liquidated," I remember a fellow *bagnard* crying out to me, "it will be liquidated and we're all going home!" Well, it was liquidated, bit by bit, piece by piece: the food, the supplies, the clothing, the furniture, every stick of administration property. And at what a price! "Come on," a friend of mine said to me on another occasion, "come on, let's go liquidate something today!" Another camp was being closed down and you had to move fast, sack in hand, to get in on the looting. And so, after a while, a few months, a few years, it was all gone. The Committee of Liquidation (and Theft) was disbanded and a curious stillness fell gradually over the *bagne*. In St. Laurent, where I was then living in a small cottage and barely managing to eke out an existence with my art, the paint began to peel off the walls of the buildings and grass began to grow in the streets. At first glance it seemed as if the liquidation had been complete, applying not only to the *bagne* but to all of Guiana as well.

But the *bagne* was not over then and it is not over now. For us it will never be over. I was one of perhaps 400 ex-convicts who had chosen not to return to France (the system of *doublage* had died with the abolition of the penal colonies) and in us the *bagne* lived and lives on. The Committee of Liquidation had been thorough, but it could not and had not liquidated the men, the living souls of the *bagnards*. We lingered on, in St. Laurent, in Cayenne, in a few of the coastal towns, a few hundred of us here and there to remind the state

What did the government do to rehabilitate the men who had served their time? It allowed them to lie down in the streets.

of its past and its present. Liquidation? No. *We* are left, *we*
are here, and what did our government do about us? The answer, of course, is nothing.

I had my work to do and I suffered less than the others. It
was during this period that I completed my series of pictures
on the *bagne*. I was not eating very well, but at least I was
eating. I had few complaints. But as I had not been indifferent to the horrors of Colonel Djibouti's regime, so I could not
now be blind or insensitive to the suffering of my fellow
bagnards left behind by the Committee of Liquidation to rot
in the streets of St. Laurent. While I painted my pictures of a
life that was no more, I also observed and later sketched out
the portraits of dozens of forgotten men. These men, many of
them, are still alive today, still with us, still unliquidated. In
Cayenne, in St. Laurent, you can see them any day, in any
street, in any doorway. It's not hard to avoid them. You have
only to cross the street, to look the other way. And why not?
It's what everyone else does. They are, after all, the mere
ghosts of a time that was and is no longer. Perhaps you have
seen one of them, as I remember seeing one of them. Here is
his portrait:

Under a torrential rain, a man in rags, a sack on his back,
comes slowly down the street. It is early morning and no one is
about. The shutters of the houses and shops are still closed
and the only sound is the clamor of the rain beating down upon
the metal roofs of the town. The man stops at each doorway,
places his sack on the ground, and leans over to make a careful
inspection of the garbage cans and boxes of rubbish that have
not yet been emptied and collected by the trucks of the sani-
tation department. His search is slow and thorough. From
time to time his hand emerges with a bottle, always empty,
which he carefully puts into his own sack. When he is sure

that each garbage can, each box of trash has no more treasures to yield, the man picks up his sack and moves on.

His face is long, thin, sickly looking, but he chooses to hide it behind a full, shaggy, white beard that gives him, at first glance, an oddly distinguished appearance. This impression is quickly dispelled by his eyes, which are dark, blank, and focused inwardly, on oblivion. He is tall, skeletal, and moves as if he might at any moment crumble into dust. His trousers are of canvas, once blue, now green, pierced and torn in a thousand places, held together by a frayed rope; his sandals have survived against incredible odds and cling to his feet because they have nowhere else to go; his shirt is hardly that, a mere rag with holes from which his arms, terrifyingly emaciated, white, and hairless, emerge obscenely; his beret is blue, dark blue, and it sits on his head of gray hair as if grown for the purpose. He is a *clochard*, a derelict, a wreck, a corpse, and not worth a second glance.

When he has finished his morning's search and his sack contains its quota of treasures, the man disappears around a corner. Wait there for him, don't move. In a few minutes he returns. The sack is empty and now you can rest assured that Armand (for even derelicts have names) has earned his day's keep. Don't smile. Go your way. Later, perhaps, you will see him again. This time he will be asleep. You will find him on some street corner, his head beneath the sack or on it, and somewhere in the vicinity you will also notice an empty discarded tin can and, more significant, another in his collection of bottles, this one empty, too, but reeking strongly of *tafia*. Armand will have found the oblivion he has been seeking. . . .

Who is Armand? Or rather, who was he? During the years of the *bagne* he was known as *le beau Charlie*, the name he carried into prison life from his world of inverted pleasures. *Le beau Charlie* had murdered his chauffeur and also the man with whom his chauffeur, an ungrateful lover, had betrayed him. A crime of passion. Armand expiated it by serving twenty years on the *Îles du Salut,* in silence, with the austerity of a gentleman, the uncomplaining acceptance of an ex-officer. He was reprieved, as many of us were, at the time of the liquidation. He walked out into the freedom he had not wanted and not asked for with a determination to find for himself the oblivion that had been, as it turned out, only temporarily imposed upon him by the *bagne.*

Without employment, without a place to live, without money, friendless and deprived by age and prison life of his beauty, he soon became a typical derelict, finding in alcohol his only salvation. At first he worked here and there, doing odd jobs about the hospital and the post office, but the money he made was spent at once and entirely on drink and soon the jobs were no longer even offered to him. He found his solution in garbage and trash, reaping his precious daily harvest of bottles from them. Money to this ex-millionaire no longer meant anything and he spent his few sous on *tafia,* the means to oblivion. The street became his home, the garbage can his office. He sleeps where he falls, under the rain or out of it, sharing his sleeping quarters with pigs and stray dogs and the rats that roam the open sewers by night.

How can an educated and intelligent man from a good background become such a wreck? We can search for the reasons in the criminal character of the man himself, in his weaknesses and vices, but who among us is entirely free from such human frailties? Can we not also find reasons in the years of imprisonment, in the brutalizing treatment the man received day in, day out for two decades? Can we not find reasons in the attitude of a judiciary that often makes no distinction between the premeditated crime and the psychological aberration of the individual? Is no blame to be attached to the indifference of a society that defends itself by making of the victimizing criminal merely another victim?

Apart from restoring their freedom to them, what has been done for these human wrecks? Is it with the few hundred francs they have been able to earn during twenty or thirty years of imprisonment that we expect them to rehabilitate themselves? Perhaps it would have been better if, once freed, they had all had the grace to die, as many of the men who chose to return to France did. There, enfeebled by the abrupt change of climate and diet, at the mercy of big-city slum life, the old *bagnards* succumbed quickly. Unfortunately, those of us who chose to remain in Guiana were ungrateful enough to live on.

Armand would not return to France. He was urged to, but he obstinately refused. He was no longer much of a man, but he was still human enough not to wish to shame himself and his surviving relatives by reappearing in a world that had forgotten him and considered him among the dead. Nor did he wish to thrust himself upon the charity either of the state or of his own family. He chose to remain in Guiana. And what did that choice offer him? What road was open to him? What hand was raised to help him? No choice, no road, no hand. Misery and oblivion were his lot, as it has become the lot of so many other old *bagnards*.

You can see them today, tonight, in the streets and alleys and doorways of Cayenne and St. Laurent. They will be sitting or lying down, usually motionless, perhaps asleep, rescued from themselves by the precious *tafia*. Perhaps they are happy. Perhaps they are philosophers in their own right. Once I went to one of them who seemed to be in some pain and I said, "Come on, my friend, come with me to the hospital." The man shook his head and answered, "The hospital? Why the hospital? Better to lie in the street." Yes, perhaps of all of us who have served our time in the *bagne,* Armand's solution is the best one. In a way, I admire him. Better indeed to lie in the street.

21 The Last Fling

UNLIKE Armand and most of my fellow *lib-érés*, I did not have the grace to lie down in the street. My old resilience asserted itself and I adapted as well as I could to the new order of things. Though I was a free man, I was well aware that I was more than ever an outcast, at least from the well-to-do everyday world of the French bourgeois, but I tried not to let my situation bother me. After all, I had always been an outcast from that world, so I did not let it upset me. Among the *Créoles* I was, of course, accepted and I lived in harmony among them. My only serious preoccupation was getting enough to eat and keeping a roof over my head, no easy matter at that time in St. Laurent. With the *bagne* gone and general poverty the order of the day, there was little call for the services of an artist. Nevertheless, I managed to scrape along and stay alive. There were days, many of them, when I did not eat; there were weeks when I fell behind in my rent, but I survived them and continued to work.

I don't want to exaggerate or to make excuses for myself. There is, after all, nothing heroic about poverty and others suffered much more than I. But I do want it to be understood that it was an ugly time for everyone and that we were all, to some extent, embittered by what had been done to us. I make no excuses for what happened; I merely state the facts. By now it should have been established that I am no knight in armor and that I always respond to difficulties by seeking a way, however devious, out of them. By 1949, after three years of scraping along from day to day, from one small job to another, one bad meal to the next, I was ready for a change. I wanted most of all to leave Guiana, to go preferably to Mexico, where I wanted to work among the native muralists, the finest in the world. Mural painting had always been a secret ambition of mine, but I had never been able to envision a way of achieving it. Mainly, however, I wanted to leave St. Laurent and the misery of its streets. Naturally, I needed money and there was no money to be had. I was willing to listen to almost any offer, reasonable or not, and, inevitably, an offer was made.

One day a man named John Wurst came to see me. I knew him only casually, well enough to exchange greetings with him in the street, but I knew something about him. He was a *Créole* of Dutch-English descent, about forty, very dark, heavily built, with a round, shining head and a wide, rather unpleasant-looking mouth. Though a citizen of Surinam, he lived in St. Laurent, where he ran a small, not very successful garage service. I knew, however, that his real profession was smuggling; he ran pirogues full of contraband back and forth in a two-way traffic across the Maroni. His activities did not make him in any way unusual at the time, since it was then well-known that half the population of St. Laurent participated in them, and Wurst was only a small-time operator in the traffic. He talked a big game, but he had never impressed me as being particularly resourceful or intelligent.

I was surprised to see him and I was even more surprised by what he had to say to me. He strolled into the small, nar-

row room I used as a studio, nodded to me, and came right to
the point. "Lagrange," he said, "I know all about you."

"You do? What do you know?"

John Wurst smiled and put a finger to his nose, as if only
he possessed some crucial knowledge about me. "I know that
you used to make money, perfect money."

"Get to the point."

"I want you to make some money for me. Lots of it," John
Wurst said. "We'll split. What do you say?"

"I don't say anything," I answered. "*You* keep talking."

John Wurst's proposition was remarkably simple. He
wanted me to make counterfeit Dutch bank notes which he
proposed to exchange in Surinam. We would divide the profits
equally. "It's easy, Lagrange," he said. "They don't expect this
kind of thing in this part of the world. Anyway, there's no
risk involved. I'll do all the changing and you won't even be in
the country. Now what do you say?"

"Let me see the bills you want."

John Wurst smiled broadly, reached into his wallet, and produced a hundred-florin note. "There," he said. "No need to
make any of the others. I can change as many of these as I
want."

"You can?"

"Certainly," he said. "It's a big enough bill to make us a lot
of money quickly, but not so big that anyone could get suspicious, you see?"

Silently, I took the bill from him and examined it. John
Wurst fidgeted impatiently and waited for me to say something. Finally, he could stand it no longer and interrupted
my inspection of the bill. "Well, Lagrange?" he said. "Come
on, you know it's a setup. We'll make a killing."

I turned the bill over and over in my hands. "Yes," I said, "a killing for a lifetime."

John Wurst did not catch my double meaning. "You *will* do it!" he said. "I *knew* you would!"

I looked up at him, at that face full of confidence and greed, and I thought back to the man I had been, back over nearly twenty years to the life I had once had, to the people I had once known, to the days and nights of my own high, good times. Then I looked away from John Wurst and around the dingy, discolored walls of the miserable little room we were in. My eye fell on the only table in that room, a rickety affair covered with paint brushes, half-empty cans of paint, dirty dishes and glasses, crumpled pieces of paper and bits of string. As I gazed with distaste at this debris, a large cockroach crawled nonchalantly across it, undoubtedly a fat scout from the hordes that infested the building.

"Well?" John Wurst said, shifting his feet impatiently.

I folded the bank note and put it in my pocket. "Get me a few clean ones," I said. "I'll keep this one for now, but I can't work from it."

John Wurst nearly went through the ceiling in his ecstasy. "Of course, of course, Lagrange," he babbled. "Anything else?"

"Plenty," I said. "Have you got the paper?"

"That's the whole idea," John Wurst said. "I have about 500 pounds of the stuff."

"Good. I'll have to make the plates. Got a place to work? I won't do it here."

John Wurst nodded. "My garage," he said. "Upstairs. There's not a chance anyone will walk in on you."

"You make sure of that."

"I will, I will!"

"It'll take me some time," I said. "These bills aren't easy. When can I start?"

"Today!"

"Tomorrow will do," I said. "Now, about the denominations —do you think we ought to try only this one note?"

"Why waste our time with others?" John Wurst said. "This is just the right note. And then we're not going to keep it up forever, are we? One big killing and out. All right?"

"Exactly my idea," I said calmly. "Now, Wurst, you won't change your mind on that? It will be a big temptation. And once started, it's hard to stop."

"You can count on me, Lagrange. Just one big killing, that's all."

"I'll hold you to it," I said.

John Wurst bounded for the door. "I'll see you tomorrow then."

"Just a minute."

He turned back.

"How many people are in on this and who are they?"

"No one's in on it," John Wurst said, beaming. "Just you and me." Again he started for the door. "Oh, my wife knows," he added, with an apologetic little smile.

"What's the penalty for counterfeiting in Surinam?" I asked.

John Wurst looked puzzled, even slightly distressed. "I don't . . . I don't know," he said.

"Maybe you'd better find out," I said to him. "It's better to know these things in advance. . . ."

"Oh. Oh, yes," he said and rushed out.

Two months later, John Wurst left St. Laurent for an extended business trip in Surinam. With him went 7,000,000 florins, all in one hundred-florin notes. Being a little out of practice, I had had a good deal of difficulty making these bills; in fact, I had had to destroy ten or twelve plates before I was able to turn out even a respectable-looking note. Eventually, however, I made a really excellent plate and began turning out perfect bills. John Wurst had been out of his mind with excitement and I had only with difficulty been able to restrain him from rushing right away into Surinam with small batches of notes. "There's no sense making any trial runs," I had said to him. "With this operation we make one big killing, remember?" John Wurst had nodded and assured me that he remembered very well. On the morning he left, I went back to my studio to resume my painting and to wait.

I waited three months, during which time I heard nothing at all from my partner. The first few weeks I thought nothing of it. I knew that it would take some time to change the notes; it would have been too risky to dump them all at once into circulation. However, three months seemed a little bit too long and the silence seemed a little bit too complete. I paid *Madame* Wurst a visit.

She was a short, fat *Créole* who had once probably been attractive, but life with John Wurst had not been kind to her and she had escaped from it by eating. I found her in the kitchen, disappearing into an enormous bowl of rice. "Good evening, *Madame*," I said to her. "I hope you are well?"

Madame grunted noncommittally and immersed herself more deeply in her meal.

"I was wondering, *Madame*," I said, "whether there has been any word of your husband? It's been quite a long time."

Madame chewed heavily, thoughtfully, magnificently. She swallowed her mouthful and prepared to attack another one. During this time she did not so much as glance at me and I was wondering whether she was even aware of my presence.

I was about to speak again when *Madame* suddenly looked up at me, her spoon poised above the heaping bowl. "That bastard," she said, "you gave him all the money, did you? Well, you won't see him again and neither will I." And she swooped down upon the rescuing rice.

A week or so later I told a friend of mine, who was going for a short visit to Paramaribo, to make some casual inquiries about John Wurst. When my friend got back, he stopped in to see me. "I didn't have any trouble finding out about this Wurst," he told me. "Apparently he used to live in Paramaribo and just recently moved back there. Everyone's very impressed with him because he never used to amount to much and now he seems to have all the money in the world. He's bought himself a large garage and a whole fleet of American cars, about ten of them. I guess he's pretty successful. He's been seen around town with a lot of very beautiful women. That's about all I found out about him, Flag. Is that what you wanted to hear?"

"Not exactly," I said, "but it will have to do. Thank you."

After my friend had gone, I went to the mirror and had a good laugh on myself. There's nothing in the world more comical than a trickster tricked and at that moment I enjoyed the unenviable status of being the biggest fool in town. Well, I said to myself, John Wurst may not have much in the way of brains, but he seems to be heavily endowed compared to you.

I was in a fine spot. In an excess of caution and folly, I had even destroyed my plates, so that now there was no way for me even to risk a solo venture with my own large batch of counterfeit bills. Nevertheless, I decided to go at once to Surinam. I did have about 30,000 florins' worth of fake notes and I thought I might as well change what I had. Also, I was hoping that word of my presence in the country would force John

Wurst into some sort of division of the spoils. I knew there was no longer any hope of getting my full share, but I did feel that I might arrive in time to be able to command a sizable portion of it. I was not yet ready to admit defeat; having decided to benefit from one last fling at crime, I was not going to allow anyone like John Wurst to rob me of all the booty.

Despite the fact that I had no passport and, as an ex-convict, no immediate prospect of getting one (John Wurst must have counted heavily on my inability to embarrass him with my presence), I crossed the Maroni at night by pirogue and once again found myself in the neat, pleasant streets of Albina. From there I wrote John Wurst a letter, friendly in tone, informing him that I had come to Surinam on business, to decorate a small café in Albina, but that I expected to see him shortly in Paramaribo. I didn't want to frighten him either with threats or by an unexpected confrontation; I wanted merely to inform him of my quiet determination to seek an accounting and at the same time give him a few days to think things over and get himself ready to part with some of his fortune. I was certain he would see the light. Better a settling with me than running the risk of losing everything.

I planned to remain in Albina for a couple of weeks, during which time I would change the money I had brought with me. I had rented a small room in a private house, set myself up as an artist at work, and even begun to make some drawings of the waterfront area. Meanwhile, I went about quietly changing my fake bills. My system was simple. I would walk into a store, buy a few florins' worth of merchandise, give the storekeeper a hundred-florin note, and pocket the change. There was little risk involved, so long as I was careful not to overdo it; the trick was not to buy too much or too often in any one place. Unfortunately, Albina is a small town and I had changed only a small amount of money by the time I was ready to make a second go-around. Nevertheless, I had spaced my visits carefully and kept track of their order; I was confident that I risked nothing by making another tour. I was in for the shock of my life.

One of the very first stores I had entered had been a dark, rather dingy little pharmacy run, as most of the stores in French Guiana and Surinam are, by a Chinese family. The sons, daughters, and minor relatives took turns waiting on customers, but the cash drawer was presided over by the chief of the tribe. He was an ancient mandarin with a heavily wrinkled face, a wispy white beard and mustache, and the hooded eyes of an exhausted, terribly cynical old bird of prey. As far as I could tell, he never moved from his perch, a high stool, above the day's receipts and, when I made my second foray into his domain, he never even so much as acknowledged my presence by a glance or a nod. To tell the truth, I had paid very little attention to him on my previous visit. He had accepted my money unquestioningly and I saw no reason to suspect difficulties this time. I went about my business with confidence.

When I had acquired a pack of razor blades and a small bottle of cologne, I presented myself before him, showed him the goods, and handed him one of my notes. The old mandarin accepted it without a word, opened his drawer, put my bill into a compartment, and gave me my change. I thanked him and started for the door, absent-mindedly counting the small bills and coins as I went. I quickly realized that there had been a mistake and, with an apologetic smile, I turned back and again confronted my inscrutable antagonist.

"Excuse me, *Monsieur*," I said, "I believe there has been a mistake."

The old Chinaman fixed me with those odd, hooded eyes of his. "Yes?" he said very softly.

"You see, *Monsieur,* I have just bought the razor blades and the small bottle of cologne," I said, holding them out for his inspection. "I believe that comes to twelve florins."

The Chinaman nodded once very slowly. "Correct," he said.

"Then I should have had eighty-eight florins back," I said. Again the old Chinaman nodded.

"Ah, but you see, *Monsieur,*" I said, showing him my change, "you have given me only forty-four florins."

This time the old man merely gazed at me for several seconds; his face was absolutely expressionless. Finally, he spoke. "Fifty-fifty," he said, ever so softly.

I must have stood there for a full minute. I was speechless, paralyzed, my mouth agape. The old Chinaman merely sat on his stool and stared at me mildly. At last, without another word, I pocketed my change and almost ran out of the store.

To this day I don't know how that old man spotted my bills as counterfeit. After I had left his store, I shut myself up in my room and carefully scrutinized every one of them. I couldn't spot a single flaw. Of course, there was nothing for me to do now but to change all my bills in his store. This simplified matters for me to some extent, but it made me a nervous wreck and cut short my stay in Albina.

After my last exchange with the old man, I made an attempt to wrench the secret from him. "Please," I said, whispering so there would be no chance of anyone overhearing us, "how did you know?"

But that old vulture could not be shaken. All he did was contemplate me with his usual mild, indifferent stare. "Know?" he said. "Know what, *Monsieur?*"

I decided not to push my luck and I walked out of his store.

My surprise partnership with the old gentleman had cost me nearly 12,000 florins.

Another surprise was in store for me in Paramaribo. I left for the capital, as I had so many years before, on the coastal steamer *Princess Juliana* and, when I arrived, I was again met at the dock by a correct, impeccably attired police officer. It was no longer my old friend Kleinhod, but his successor, a younger, equally impressive official named Vickers. As I stepped ashore, he clicked his heels and bowed. "*Monsieur* Lagrange?" he said in excellent French. "Please come with me, if you don't mind."

I did mind, but I had no choice. I realized at once that something was seriously wrong and, seated in a comfortable chair in Chief Vickers's office, I soon found out what it was. "Two days ago," Chief Vickers said to me, "we arrested a man named John Wurst. He was caught passing counterfeit bills, all in hundred-florin notes. Do you know this man?"

"Yes," I said. "Only slightly. He owns a small garage in St. Laurent, I believe."

"The truth, Lagrange, the truth!" Chief Vickers said, tapping the top of his desk impatiently.

"You think I made the bills for him, is that it?"

"Of course. We know you did."

"You'll have to prove that, *Monsieur.*"

It wasn't hard. From what Vickers told me that morning and what I knew of Wurst, I was easily able to piece the story together. My wretched partner had been thrown into a panic by my letter and the news of my arrival in Albina. He didn't fear my vengeance or anything silly like that, but he had not yet changed all of his money and he had no desire to make any sort of split with me. He reasoned that I must have brought my own counterfeit bills into Surinam and he feared a flooding

of the market. Not content with what he had and unwilling
to part with any of it, he made a reckless attempt to complete
his big coup before I could arrive on the scene. In other words,
he was undone by his greed as well as by his stupidity.

The system he chose was unique in its imbecility. Afraid
to change any more bills in Paramaribo and anxious to avoid
at all costs an encounter with me, he left the capital and began
a rapid journey through the interior villages of Surinam. Everywhere he went he changed his hundred-florin notes. His
method was the one I had used, or had intended to use, in
Albina, but inevitably John Wurst abused it. After having
rapidly changed all of his fake bills, he went back through the
same villages reconverting his smaller denominations and coins
into hundred-florin notes, probably because he intended to flee
the country and found it difficult to travel with so much money
in bulk. This was stupid enough, but John Wurst embellished
his stupidity with a final typically moronic touch. Because he
was afraid that the unwitting storekeepers would give him
back some of the fake bills, he refused to accept any hundred-
florin notes until he could check their serial numbers against
the list of numbers he had written down in a small pocket notebook that he carried around with him, from transaction to
transaction! I had no trouble imagining the expression on the
face of the first storekeeper whose hundred-florin notes had
just been rejected by the very man who had given them to
him a day or two previously.

John Wurst had been arrested and brought back to Paramaribo. At first he had denied any knowledge of the crime,
claiming that he had been given the bills by an old Frenchman in St. Laurent, who had asked him to change them for
him. However, in his pocket the police had found the incrimi-

nating notebook; in addition to the serial numbers, it included my name and address. Good old John Wurst!

"Well, *Monsieur* Lagrange," Chief Vickers said to me, "is there any need to go on denying everything? Must we confront you with this man Wurst?"

"You have the notebook, of course?"

"Of course." Chief Vickers opened a drawer in his desk and produced the notebook, a small, dark-brown leather affair. "Would you like to see it?"

"No need," I said with a sigh. "No need."

The Dutch police turned out to be much gentler and more trusting than the French and Germans I had known. Instead of being locked up at once in a cell, I was merely placed into protective custody in a private apartment close to the police station, and though I was watched day and night, I was allowed the run of the town while awaiting trial. I never saw John Wurst, because a few days after my arrest he escaped and disappeared into the bush, and it was four months before he was recaptured.

Despite the fact that both Wurst and I had confessed our guilt, the case was complicated by the incredulity of one of the examining magistrates, a certain Judge Millberg. This old bearded veteran of the criminal courts simply couldn't believe that I had actually manufactured the counterfeit notes as I said I had; he insisted that both Wurst and I were lying, that we were probably covering up for a much larger operation with its origins back in Europe. There seemed to be only one way to convince Judge Millberg that I was telling the truth; I volunteered to make him some more fake hundred-florin notes. "You must order me to do so, Your Honor," I said to him, "or I shall have to refuse. I certainly don't want to incriminate myself a second time in your eyes."

"No, no, Lagrange," the judge said. "This will be only a demonstration. I shall take into consideration during the trial your desire to co-operate with this court."

The authorities provided me with the necessary materials and a room in which to work. Within a week I had turned out twenty-three bills that looked perfect to me and I informed Judge Millberg that I was ready.

The demonstration took place in a large reception room of the City Hall, and there were about eighty people present, including many high officials of the government and the police, as well as a number of newspaper reporters. The director of the Bank of Surinam, a portly, serious-looking gentleman with a goatee and a pince-nez, supervised the test. He mixed twenty of my bills with fifty real ones and placed all the notes into a large envelope. The envelope was passed around the room and people were asked to identify the counterfeit notes. Only one man, a young Chinese lawyer, was able to single out one of my bills and I immediately saw why: a drop of acid had slightly smudged a line in one corner of the note and the hawk-eyed Chinaman had spotted it. (The Chinese, I concluded, were evidently infallible judges of money!) But with this one exception, no one in the room was able to distinguish the real money from the false, until the director of the bank was able to make the proper division by checking the serial numbers of the real bills.

The effect of the demonstration was most curious. Overnight I became a celebrity. The newspapers played up the story on their front pages, including in all the dramatic accounts photographs of myself and of the contest. Everywhere I went, people pointed me out. Very often they would come up and shake my hand, pat my back, and congratulate me, as if I had accomplished something very tremendous and worthy.

Even Chief Vickers was lavish in his praise. Judge Millberg, when he had recovered from his astonishment, summoned me to his private office. "Lagrange," he said to me, after a rather mild lecture on the evils and perils of dishonest living, "how could a man of your character and ability have formed a partnership with a hoodlum like Wurst? I'm ashamed of you, Lagrange!"

I don't know exactly how much this demonstration and my new fame contributed to the peculiar end of this episode of my life, my very last venture into crime. I am certain that psychologically it contributed considerably. I had struck some deep, hidden spot in the human animal, some area in which man hides his secret feelings about life or society. The fact is that people were delighted to hear that one man, working humbly and alone, could outwit the entire cumbersome apparatus of the state. Everyone of us, I suspect, nourishes certain secret resentments against society and the power that it wields over all of us, compelling us to bow to its will and to play the game by its own dishonest rules, and we are ready to rejoice and cheer the exploits of the man who defies or outwits this enemy.

I was also helped by my lawyer's brilliant defense. This man, assigned personally by Judge Millberg to represent me during the trial, discovered an odd aspect of the Dutch law on counterfeiting. This law dates back to 1745 and is written in the peculiar language and according to the peculiar situations of the day. At that time a convicted counterfeiter could be sentenced to death, but only if he were a citizen of Holland; a foreigner could only be escorted to the frontier and told not to return. When the law was changed and the maximum penalty for counterfeiting in Dutch territory was established at nine years' imprisonment, some of the original wording of the law was retained and incorporated into the new act, enough of it, my lawyer claimed, to cast serious doubt on the competence of the Dutch court to sentence me to anything more drastic than extradition. I was, after all, a French citizen.

I doubt whether this curious argument would have stood up against a judge determined to sentence me to jail, but Judge Millberg was ready, even eager to accept it. I received a stern lecture on morality and I was condemned to immediate deportation!

In looking back over my life, nothing seems stranger to me than my recurrent fate of always, for so many different reasons and on so many different occasions, being sent back to St. Laurent. I realized at last, as the boat from Albina again approached the French bank of the Maroni, that I was destined never to escape French Guiana, not even as a free man.

As for John Wurst, I am happy to say that, after his recapture, he was brought to trial and sentenced to nine years in jail. One of the few happy endings of my life.

22 Cayenne

MY last return to St. Laurent was anything but triumphant, even though I was not being sent back to imprisonment. The French authorities had followed my adventures in Surinam with considerable interest and they must have been both indignant and astounded by the outcome. No sooner had I landed than I was summoned to appear before the chief of police, a thin, dried-up little man with a waspish voice and temper.

"Lagrange," he said to me, "you can make fools out of the Dutch blockheads but not out of me. Now I'll tell you what we're going to do, Lagrange. You're going to keep your nose clean or I'm going to send you back to jail. As long as you are in St. Laurent, you will report every day to this office and give a full accounting of your activities. If you fail to report every single day, Lagrange, I'm going to find a means of putting you away for good. I hope that's clear. Get out."

It was very clear. If I remained in St. Laurent, I would once again fall into the clutches of the penal system, perhaps even be returned to France. When I went home, for example, I discovered that my bungalow had been ransacked, all but destroyed by the rough methods of the local police investigators.

Life in St. Laurent was going to become intolerable and dangerous for me. I decided that there was nothing for me to do but scrape some money together and move to Cayenne, where presumably I would be left in comparative peace.

It was two years before I was able to make such a move and during that time I sweated to remain out of trouble. It wasn't easy because I was quite literally hounded morning and afternoon by the police. The situation improved somewhat the second year with the arrival of a new civil administration, but it was a delicate, dangerous time in my life.

Finally, I was able to move to Cayenne and I have lived here ever since. The days, the months, the years have passed without incident and my life has not been an unhappy one. I have supported myself by my work, what I call my "shop work"—portraits painted on order, souvenir scenes of French Guiana, decorative pictures for the tourist trade, what there is of it— and I have also found the time to paint. I am not rich, but I get along from day to day. I have many friends and I have had several love affairs. By the *Créoles* I have been accepted absolutely, if not by the stuffier members of the white community. I have my books, a good radio, an occasional movie. I used to take long walks around the picturesque town, but lately I have begun to feel my years and I now prefer to spend much of my leisure time sipping an *apéritif* with my friends at one of the sidewalk tables of *le snack bar*. My friends also like to drop in on me, but I try to discourage them. Too often they appear when I am working, which disrupts the routine of my day and makes me nervous and irritable. I am moderately happy and I have few complaints.

Like all the other *bagnards*, I live, too, with the memory of the *bagne*, with the ghosts of old faces and the echoes of old voices. I had shut the past out with some success until the reappearance of Paul Bonnard, but now it can no longer be denied. I face it without regrets, with no apologies, even with a certain amount of pleasure. After all, unlike so many other men, respectable men, I have *lived*. I have known wealth and love and adventure and laughter. There is little more, I think, to living than these few simple joys.

To the good citizens of Guiana I am still a *bagnard,* one of *les vieux blancs,* as we are known to them. (I also have the reputation of a Don Juan, wholly undeserved because, unlike my famous predecessor, I have been and still am an imbecile when it comes to women.) I expect that this will never change, and why should it? I am what I am and what I have made myself. At least I am not alone. Today, in Cayenne, we are still perhaps a hundred strong. It's impossible to get any exact count because the government, having abolished the *bagne,* would prefer to forget that it ever existed at all. Journalists who arrive here and ask embarrassing questions are not welcome. The civil officials will tell them that there are hardly any of the old convicts left, a dozen in all perhaps, that the *bagne* is not even a memory.

And yet, oddly enough, despite the liquidation and the government's anxiety to forget, the *bagne* lingers on. In addition to those of us who were once part of it, there are today in Cayenne a few men, thirty or forty in all, who are still serving sentences. They live in the local jail and work during the day as servants for government officials and their wives, just as in the old days. You can see them any day in the streets of the town. They are no longer dressed in the old striped costume of the *bagne,* but they are *bagnards* just the same. The government may wish to forget, but it cannot, any more than we can, obliterate the reality of the prison system. Wherever there is a prison, there you find a *bagnard.*

Do I regret what I have done? No. And why not? Because I have paid for it with my life. Am I incorrigible? Yes, undoubtedly. I am an artist and a bit of a rogue. I know this about myself and I see no reason to hide it. Would I do it all again? Most certainly, though I would wish, I think, to remain truer to myself as an artist than I have been. I can speak with some confidence because, not long ago, I was sitting at my usual place outside *le snack bar*. The sun was warm, the sky blue above, and I felt suddenly young, very much alive, and the man I once was. With me and two other men was a young, very beautiful *Créole* girl named Arianne. She was not more than twenty, full of life and laughter and the surging joy of wishing to be somewhere else, somewhere gayer and brighter than Cayenne. For some minutes she had been complaining, expressing a desire to escape Guiana, to return to Paris where she had once lived with her family for several years. "Then why don't you go?" I said to her.

Arianne smiled, such a beautiful smile, such white teeth against the dark brown of her skin, and she said, "Flag, how can I? I have no money."

And all I could do was laugh and lean across the table to pat her lovely little hand. "Then, my dear," I said to her, meaning every word of it, "then you must come to me and I will make you some!"